DEDICATED TO

Paul, my soulmate and love of my life

&

Kalin: our beginning

Shawn: our continuation

Michael: our culmination

Kathy Kenney-Marshall is a wife, mother of three, and a self-professed word nerd. She finds humor in most things, including the drama of her third-grade classroom and the tumult and joy that is family. She even finds humor in of all places, the operating room! Her columns have appeared in the MetroWest Daily News *since 2003 and her children's poetry can be found in seven anthologies published by Meadowbrook Press. She lives in a suburb of Boston.*

Praise for
Kathy Kenney-Marshall's
"Crumbs from
the Table of Life"

"Kathy Kenney-Marshall has been a valued contributor to the *MetroWest Daily News* opinion pages for years. As a teacher and a writer, she's shown an ability to reach both children and adults, to find humor all ages can appreciate, and to help people who are generations apart get on the same page."

Rick Holmes
Editor, MetroWest Daily News

"Kathy Kenney-Marshall loves language, stories, and M&Ms. As an excellent teacher and writer, Kathy Kenney-Marshall is an astute observer of the landscape of everyday life. Her columns reflect her wit, passion, and insight into the human condition. Whether she's writing about the classroom, her family, or the mundane routines that keep us all busy, Kenney-Marshall always cuts through the morning fog and shines a little afternoon sunlight on how we tend to our business. Her writing points to the essential truths of daily life: it's difficult and challenging, but always an interesting ride."

Andrew Green
Founder, Potato Hill Poetry

"Don't be fooled. Kathy Kenney-Marshall may claim to offer *Crumbs from the Table of Life,* but her words are food for the soul."

Eric Ode
Author and Award-Winning Songwriter

Dan, the Taxi Man, Kane Miller
When You're a Pirate Dog and Other Pirate Poems, Pelican Publishing
Tall Tales of the Wild West (And a Few Short Ones), Meadowbrook Press

"I've known KKM for years — as someone who publishes the poetry she writes for children and as someone who enjoys reading her columns — when she's kind enough to send them to me. Kathy has a wonderful sense of humor combined with a truth-telling instinct from her perspective as a mother and a teacher. It's always a pleasure to read her latest column, hot off the press."

Bruce Lansky
Publisher, Meadowbrook Press

Contents

Crumbs from the Parental Plate 3

An Icebox Covered in Memories 4
Coming Home: A Bittersweet Reunion 6
Driving Miss Mommy 8
Family Vacations 12
Front Porch Stories 14
Getting Ready for College 16
Grampa's Car 18
Hiding Things Where They Belong: A Lost Art Form 20
Holiday Traditions Are Worth Waiting For 22
A Little Hope under the Tree 26
Is Lying Just a Part of Growing Up? 28
Learning How to Train Your Child 30
Fumble or Touchdown? 32
Christmas Memories Last Longer Than a Day 34
Picking Favorites 37
Pretty in the City or Slacker Mom? 40
Reality in Reality Television 44
The Pain and Pride of Leaving Home 46
The Breast-feeding Debate Lives On 48
When Crime Hits Home 50
Getting through the Teenage Years 52
Mother of the Year 54

Crumbs from the Classroom 57

Lifelong Learning: The Greatest Gift 58
Class Pests and Pets 61
The First Year 66
The Thing about Kellie 68
Captain Underpants: More Than Just a Funny Book 72
A Noble Endeavor 76
Headlights and Homework 82
Dear Matchbooks 84
Healthy Halloween 88
Is the Sky the Limit for Everyone? 90

Gift of Poetry in Children 92
Parent-Teacher Time 94
Reporting on Report Cards 98
Report Cards Offer the Gift of Gab 100
Third-Grade Politics 102
A Turn for the Worse 104
Liar, Liar, Pants on Fire 106

Just Plain Crumbs 111

Electronically Challenged 112
Choices Aren't Always That Easy 114
Finding Your Inner Child at Christmas 116
Getting the Hang of Hanging Out on the Curb 118
Going Back to School: A Big Deal at Any Age 122
To Gossip or Not to Gossip: A Pop Culture Conundrum 124
Grampa Joe 126
Gym Etiquette 128
Living Well through Chemistry 130
Reality Television Hits the Workplace 132
Older and Wiser 136
A Slice of Heaven and a $20,000 Lunch 138
Super-sizing: Boon or Bust? 140
Surgery: No Laughing Matter 142
Tax Amnesty: Was it Worth the Headache? 144
The Magic of Hometown Baseball 148
The Morning After 150
Choosing to See Surprises 152
The Evils of the Remote Control 154
There's a Law for *THAT?* 156
Ignorance Is Sometimes Bliss 158
Leaving It to the Experts 160

CRUMBS from the Parental Plate

An Icebox Covered with Memories
KATHY KENNEY-MARSHALL

Langston Hughes wrote, "Sometimes a crumb falls from the tables of joy. Sometimes a bone is flung. To some people, joy is given, to others, only heaven." I found this lovely poem held to my refrigerator by a "#1 Mom" magnet. It has been there as long as I remember and I don't dare throw it away because every time I read it, I smile.

Like most parents, we can no longer tell what color our refrigerator is due to hanging important stuff up on it. The poem, while only important to me, is an example. But when I tried to clean not just the front but the sides that have been covered by assorted keepsakes, I had trouble deciding what was worthy of redemption and what needed to be placed reverently in the "circular file."

There were some easy items such as the card from the Vietnam vets requesting discarded clothing and small household items. The pick up date was February 2004. I could also live with removing the Belmont Springs water delivery schedule, as we've gotten Poland Spring for three years now. The craft fair schedule sent to me by the woman who makes my family's yearly cookie dough ornament would have stayed, except it was from 2002. The 1999 school year calendar could also be removed, though it brought back memories ... it was a great class. Expired coupons for car rentals, videos, olive oil, and coral calcium were also easy to remove, as were last year's Babe Ruth All-Star roster and the sign-up sheet for a now-defunct basketball league. (I knew the league wasn't going anywhere when most words, including '*bakskitball*' were misspelled).

But there were items that I decided could not be parted with no matter how much they cluttered the fridge. Of course, the Langston Hughes poem stays along with the yellowed newspaper clipping of the *Far Side* comic where a man stands at a fence insulting cows because he is "becoming increasingly lactose intolerant." Only those of us who are forced to use rice milk can laugh at that. From time to time, though, I find myself throwing cow insults as I pass a dairy farm. The cows barely look up from chewing their cud, but somehow I feel the loss of ice cream from my diet is vindicated.

There are also many picture magnets cluttering the surface. I can never part with those even though one is of me and a student I had in class who I believe has now graduated from high school and I have forgotten her name. I just remember that she was really sweet and we had a great rapport, plus though half of my head was cut off, I was wearing a very cool outfit. The pictures of my children in various stages of growth will remain, as will a picture of my dog, my dad, and one of my mom and me sitting in a convertible on a trip to Martha's Vineyard.

The receipt for the pool liner I bought last year arguably should be removed and filed. But my fear is that I know exactly where it is now. If I move it, I will lose it. The claim tickets from last June's dry cleaning must stay as well since school has begun and I need those dressier clothes.

There are magnetic business cards from exterminators, plumbers, electricians, and the vinyl siding guy, (who knows when Paul will come to his senses and stop 'doing it himself.') There are also heavy magnetic cards from a business venture Paul embarked on that didn't work out. I had to keep those there to remind him in case he ever decides to try again to have his vegetarian wife sell meat for a home-based food service.

The $18 golf gift certificate doesn't have an expiration date, so it stays. Whether the golf course is still in operation is anybody's guess, but it's worth the few inches of space it takes up.

The Mistle Toad and Christmas Wreath magnets can stay as well. December is only a few months away and they hold up the gym schedule from 1999, and Kalin's seventh grade report card; (she made the honor roll), which deserves space, as does her bill for the coming semester, as a reminder to pay it.

The magnetic key holder that found a spot on the side is empty, but one of these days, I will have a key made for it. Though I suppose when I do, I'll have to move it to a magnetic surface outside the house.

When I finished, I realized, based on the three-and-a-half inch square of surface that my refrigerator is white, almost. But there is an unsightly scratch there. I'm sure I can find something to cover it. ◉

Coming Home: a Bittersweet Reunion

KATHY KENNEY-MARSHALL

April showers may bring May flowers, but May brings home the coeds who have been away for most of the year. As I looked forward to the return of my own coed, Kalin, I imagined our home filled with the intensity, both good and ... interesting that is my daughter. The difference this year, after her second year away, is that she has decided to take time away from the world of academia to reconfigure what is to be her future. In other words, she came back home to "find herself." I often wonder how the youth of today got lost to begin with, but seeing that this episode of "hide-and-seek" would save us thousands in tuition bills, I was able to support her decision and welcome her back with open arms (and a list of rules). No dorm style living here and so far, knock wood, the house has been cleaner at night than when I leave in the morning, mail is brought in, and phone messages are recorded (albeit cryptically on soiled napkins). I wonder how long this honeymoon homecoming will last.

What I hadn't thought much about was the fact that as she moved home, this time for good, so did her "stuff". I guess the mind is a wonderful thing at times, because I had almost forgotten the many enormous plastic bins we purchased to pack when she left. And as "stuff" has a tendency to do, it multiplied. As parents of college kids, we forget that life does, in fact, go on without us as these young adults continue to shop and collect things we don't have to look at when they are crowding a dorm room instead of our homes. Usually, by the time one graduates, they themselves have made several trips to the dumpster to erase the evidence of their "misspent youth." Not so when they come home a little earlier than planned.

As I walked into the house the other day, after a day that felt like a week, I was greeted with 87 Rubbermaid bins, almost emptied, and a mound of dirty and clean laundry that reached my bellybutton. I embellish of course ... it only reached my hips. What was missing, I came to realize after finding her sprawled on the couch one morning because there was no space left for her in her bedroom, was anything that resembled a real pair of socks. She had on two of mine ... new ... and they didn't match, either. There is, I found later that day, a pair exactly like them on the basement floor: she wore those yesterday. Apparently, college life left her colorblind.

As the week has gone by and her "stuff" has found space to occupy, I realize that my own "stuff" has been tossed aside to make way for hers. My hairdryer, not good enough for 20-year-old hair, is often left at the door of the bathroom. I think I may have to buy a new one, seeing I yet again stepped on it at 5am in my early morning stupor to the shower. I know this because it singed me as it sparked to life after I unbent the prongs of the plug before shoving it into the socket. Her dryer was tidily put into the bathroom closet where my make-up used to be. And where might my makeup have found a new home you might wonder? Behind the toilet, of course ... and there are three males in the house. Hmmmmm, should I wonder why I am developing a rash on my face?

There are good things about having another female in the house. For example, we can share razors; though yesterday I found myself nursing six cuts from a dull razor that I changed just two days ago. Usually, my razors last longer than that. We can also use each other's brushes. Funny thing though, I found my brush alongside my makeup one morning, and for some reason, I had a really bad hair day. Maybe it's her conditioner ... I hope.

Finally, there's the girl talk. With my husband and sons, if there isn't a ball or sport of some type in the conversation, I can say or request anything I want and the responses will typically include, "uh-huh, yeah, whatever you want." Though they almost always forget what they agreed to, at least they are agreeable. With a daughter, while you sometimes have an ally and an almost friendly conversation, the word that rhymes with *witch* might be thrown at any given time ... like when you ask that your own socks not be worn or that your $50 facial moisturizer be put away with the cover on after she slathers it all over her legs.

And through the nicks and cuts of shaving and of life in general, you still look sometimes when your 20-year-old daughter is asleep on the couch and think of her as you did the day you brought her home from the hospital. One day, you know she will leave you for good. It is a bittersweet thought, though my face, legs, and my hairdryer may be grateful for the space. ☻

Driving Miss Mommy

KATHY KENNEY-MARSHALL

I am a natural brunette ... honest! But times, they are a changin' as my family grows up and continues to reach milestones, both good and not-so-good, depending on where you are sitting. And sitting I was, in the passenger side of my new midlife crisis car when another milestone hit me directly in the roots ... hair roots that is.

With the many milestones being achieved in my growing family, I find that something else is popping up ... or out ... during the process. With each change in the family, I seem to be finding new gray hairs to yank out. My yanking out time of just a few minutes a week, is turning into many minutes, (I will *NOT* divulge how many), every day. Is it that the kids are growing older, or (gulp) am I? The obvious answer is that it is *THEY* who get older ... of course. I suppose many would say that I can't stay my youthful young mother-self while they grow up and move onto grown-up activities. So why do I feel the same? Other than the circles under my eyes from staying up late waiting for them at night, and the few (almost unnoticeable – *REALLY*) laugh/worry lines around my eyes and mouth, I'm still young. Right? However, the additional gray hairs that stubbornly present themselves are harder to ignore for some reason. But today, I confirmed exactly who is at fault for that. It's definitely the kids.

Nothing is more certain to bring out a gray hair or 20, than letting your child drive on the highway with you for the very first time. Although Shawn is almost 18, he does not yet have his driver's license. That's fine with me most days, unless he needs a ride home from work at 10pm when Paul and I flip a coin over who has to go pick him up. Luckily, Paul has not discovered my two-headed coin yet, so he always loses. Today, after the dramatic ending of an 18 year relationship with his pediatrician, Shawn asked if he could drive home. We live 25 miles from his office, which includes a ride down every commuter's favorite highway, Route 128. It is a rite of passage certainly, but this request brought on a desperate wish for valium (or at the very least five or six cups of chamomile tea), for reasons I will disclose publicly for the first time. I must include this very embarrassing anecdote for which I will pay dearly when he reads this to explain my anxiety: Just last summer, Shawn asked if he could move a car out of the driveway. Quite a few of his friends were over to play basketball, so in an attempt to let him save face, I nonchalantly threw him the keys, then hovered in the driveway to make sure he didn't accidentally run over one of those friends. He got in the car, turned the key, then rolled down the window to motion me over. "Which one of these things is the gas pedal?" he whispered. I thought he was trying to make me laugh, a skill at which he is extremely adept, so I played along and laughed. His face turned serious. "I'm not kidding," he responded. I knew we were in trouble. He moved the car without hurting anyone, but I swear I literally felt four or five new grays ... pop, pop, pop, pop, budding from my scalp. I realized the boy needed help. He confided to me that he felt a little more comfortable driving with me than Paul, (translation: you're a pushover, Dad's going to tell me how it is), so I took him out to a few empty parking lots to "practice." It resulted in (pop, pop, pop), several dozen new white hairs. But after driving with him a few times this fall and with having a few driving hours through the driving school, he was doing far better and never again asked the difference between the gas and brake pedals. It was a good sign. But the highway? I was a little (a lot) apprehensive as I tossed him the keys. He did great on Route 9, but as we approached the big bad scary highway, I felt the muscles in my jaw turn as hard as granite and I turned the radio up a bit so he wouldn't hear my teeth grinding. More gray hairs were taunting me, laughing at me out loud as we pulled onto the on-ramp. As he began to merge into traffic, he apparently forgot about the steering wheel because we went slightly off track into the snow bank on the side of the ramp. No problem (for his hair, mine stood on end and 15 new gray hairs began their mocking.) He corrected this, continued to look for oncoming traffic and again headed toward the snow at the side of the ramp. I couldn't help it this time. I grabbed the wheel and corrected the problem before we went careening down the embankment. 27 more gray hairs were guffawing at my

> *Nothing is more certain to bring out a gray hair or 20, than letting your child drive on the highway with you for the very first time.*

Driving Miss Mommy

position in the passenger seat. I didn't dare turn down the visor to look in the mirror. The rest of the ride went pretty well and the off ramp experience was much smoother. We made it home in one piece and though I practically plowed the boy down to get into the house for some Tension-Tamer Tea, he felt the pride of accomplishment in successfully driving on the highway for the first time.

Now as I sit here writing about the experience, drinking my tea, I am readying myself for another first; my appointment at the hairdressers for my first dye-job. Perhaps I'll go blonde. His driving test isn't until the end of January and I've heard that in light blonde hair, gray is a just little harder to detect.

Family Vacations
KATHY KENNEY-MARSHALL

When dealing with every day chaos, sometimes it's nice to go on vacation. The mere mention of the word *vacation* conjures up positive thoughts for almost everyone I know ... except for me. When I think of vacation, I think of details: what must be packed, locked, cleaned, bought, etc. And if that weren't enough to think about, the words FAMILY TOGETHERNESS loom large over the whole dirty to-do list before you can ever step out the door.

I love my family more than anything, but I must admit; there are some things families with children over the age of ... fill in the blank ... should never do unless absolutely necessary. Taking a vacation together is one of them.

Everyone expects something different from a family vacation, and usually this leads to disappointment for all. We used to go on an annual trip with friends. There were three or four families whose children were the same age as ours. This worked out really well given that we all had our own places to escape each other when we wanted privacy, and everyone, both kids and adults, had "someone to play with." As the kids got older, we stopped the tradition as teen jobs and camp life took up too much of the summer.

Our first solo Marshall vacation was a trip to Universal Studios in Florida. Our kids were then 13, 11, and 5 so this theme park vacation seemingly had something to offer for everyone. What we didn't count on was the fact that our daughter was invited to her first girl/boy party the weekend we were gone. This created her desire to be as far away from us as possible since we were ruining her life by bringing her on a Florida vacation. How dare we! Our 11-year-old son as luck would have it, had an aversion to any rides faster than the Merry-Go-Round and even on that ride, he took a stationary pony. Sharing one hotel room with three kids was oh so much fun. Thank goodness it was only a four-day trip.

Our vacation rental in Seabrook one summer also comes to mind. It was a small cottage with several bedrooms so we thought it was worth the exorbitant price for a week at the beach. The older kids, 20 and 18, could come and go with their friends, and Mike, 13, could bring his friends as well. Everyone would have a great time ... in theory.

What we didn't count on were the extra guests. Not family members or extra friends ... they were welcome. It was the colony of ants and other creepy crawly things that left us scared to go to sleep at night. It should have been a sign when we walked in and were immediately assaulted by the smell of RAID. We all tried to ignore it, but the next morning I awoke to a parade of insects coming from many directions to feast on our vacation food.

Everyone expects something different from a family vacation and usually this leads to disappointment for all.

(*Vacation food:* noun: Anything you would never eat at home, i.e.: Funyons, Cheez Whiz, Spam)

We called the landlord immediately whereupon she sent her daughter with a bag of white powder in a baggie for us to sprinkle wherever we saw the bugs. For $1800 a week, I got to sprinkle around her run-down uncared for _ _it-hole an unknown poison that could potentially blind me. As she left, she recommended that we wear masks and run quickly to the beach for six to eight hours after using the powder.

My older two children didn't spend much time there because we had never allowed them to be alone in the house overnight and that was more appealing. What they didn't know was that I called the neighborhood busybody and left my cell phone number in the event of a party.

My youngest and his friends quickly tired of the beach and wanted to spend most of their sunny days inside the arcades ... and expected us to drive them there whenever they were bored. We left the cottage on Friday; a day early to go home where not getting along wasn't so expensive.

With summer near, a beach vacation comes to mind again. In the past, temporary amnesia took over as we paid large sums of money in the name of family togetherness. As I write this column today, I'm thinking that maybe we'll get along better at the Cape. I hear the bugs aren't quite as friendly there. ◉

Front Porch Stories

KATHY KENNEY-MARSHALL

As the summer arrives and the sun stays out longer, the front porch begins to beckon us Marshalls out of our winter hibernation in front of the television. It is a place to watch neighbors walk their dogs and make sure they don't do their business on our front lawn ... (The dogs, not the neighbors). It is a place to talk on the phone on warm evenings when you don't want anyone to hear or a place to slow down and de-stress after a long hectic week.

Our house is over 100 years old and when we bought it, the farmer's porch, though saggy and unkempt was one of the main reasons we bought it. There were stairs outside the kitchen door leading to the backyard, but they were full of dry rot and peeling paint. It needed to be fixed. Paul and his brothers replaced it with a lovely 16' by 18' deck. They did it in only one weekend ... a weekend I made myself as scarce as possible to allow for brotherly bonding which included many words I didn't want my then young children to hear.

When we bought our first patio set we were sure that we would spend many hours on the new back deck watching the kids and the dog play in the fenced in back yard. What we didn't count on were the nightly shrieks of, "Ewww, Michael stepped in dog poop again!"

The front porch once again became our gathering place. We bought a few cheap resin chairs, sat together without the worry of dog doo-doo on shoes, and got to know our new neighbors.

The addition of an above ground pool made Paul start thinking about our back deck. It scares me when Paul starts thinking of home improvement projects. As any wife knows, it is never cheaper to do it on your own and of course there is the vocabulary factor when the kids are small enough to learn there are words they must never ever say even if Daddy does.

What became known as "the deck project" continued. Paul wanted to build a deck instead of erecting the aluminum one that the pool salesman tried to sell us. I decided it would be easier to let him do his thing and I disappeared once again until the deck was finished. I admit I was impressed with the design that not only wrapped around the long side of the oval pool, but included an opening and a step-up to the first new deck. Paul was content, but not for long.

We did spend some daylight hours on the new decks, but still, evenings belonged to the front porch where the resin chairs were replaced with a porch swing. As the kids were getting older, many important conversations happened there, making it an even more integral part of our family time.

Not many years after, Paul decided to enlarge the deck. This time, we stayed home and Shawn, then old enough to help by holding the wood in place, began to learn carpentry ... and a few new interjections. I like to think of the movie *"A Christmas Story"* featuring Peter Billingsley and Darren McGavin whose blasphemous profanity came out in tones loud enough to be heard, yet garbled enough to be incomprehensible. I bought a new portable stereo and blasted it so that the youngest would not yell out these words in the grocery store. We replaced the small beach chairs with lounge chairs and enjoyed Paul's creation. Some nights were even spent there, but it lacked the personality of the old front porch.

Years passed and with rapidly growing teens, we began to outgrow our house. We needed to either move or add a family room. We added a large 24-by-24-foot family room with an additional front farmer's porch. With a large slider in the back of the room, the deck project continued. Now, hopefully complete, the back deck is 48 feet long and 18 feet wide. It's a great place for a party yet it seems to lack the charm of the old front porch. It is here that we have laughed over everything and nothing. It was where we talked to our kids about every day things and important life lessons. It is where many memories have been made. It is part of what makes our house a home.

Too soon, our kids will move out and start their own families. Paul and I will sit alone on that front porch reminiscing. And when the time comes to move to a smaller place with less maintenance required, the ad will read "Front porch for sale, house included." The memories however, will move with us. ◉

Getting Ready for College
KATHY KENNEY-MARSHALL

My son, Shawn, received his first gift two days before Christmas this year. It came in the mail in a large envelope and was ignored by everyone for a whole day. With the holidays coming, I was much too busy to open anything that didn't resemble a shut-off notice or a Christmas card. I shoved this envelope in his pile of mail and methodically worked myself into the typical holiday frenzy that I swear I will not do every year. Every year, I fail. But that is why this gift lay unopened on our computer room desk until he returned from a holiday party at midnight. He was sitting there playing that exciting and ever popular computer version of Texas Hold'em when nature called. Needing some good reading material, he perused the mail pile, choosing the new *Sports Illustrated* to bring into the porcelain library when he noticed it sitting unopened underneath the magazine. It was from the Admissions Office at UMass–Dartmouth where he had applied for entrance into their Marketing Program. He quickly ripped open the package and proceeded to dance in a way he can only do in private; jumping and gyrating in publicly embarrassing ways because we were all asleep and there would be no witnesses. "*YES! YES! YES!*" were the whispered screams that woke no one as he hung this first acceptance letter on the refrigerator for Paul and me to see in the morning. When I saw it while reaching for the coffee creamer, my first reaction was similar to Shawn's though I will gyrate and jump no matter who's looking. I never quite got to the embarrassing dance
however, because just as quickly as I felt joy, I found tears were flowing down my cheeks in a most selfish yet understandable and familiar feeling of something that resembled mourning. The reality that my second child, my oldest boy, would soon be spreading his wings to fly toward his own beginning of adulthood slammed that happy pride right into the pit of my stomach.

I remembered when my daughter left home to go to college. I didn't feel this way until I was packing up her hopelessly messy room into huge Rubbermaid plastic boxes. I would shop for her dorm room necessities and find myself weeping in the aisle where the hangers hung on neat display units or sniffling in the sheet section of Linens 'n Things. The house was quieter with only two boys left in it, yes; quieter ….she is my loudest child. But I did become accustomed to being the only female in the house and actually enjoyed the fact that my hairdryer was never missing and my $40 moisturizer lasted quite a bit longer without sharing it with someone else. But I missed her laugh, I missed the arguments over the location of the tweezers, and I missed the female companionship when the boys were doing boy things that mothers are not allowed to participate in.

But that too became familiar and even acceptable as I looked forward to daily emails where we got along even better than in real person. We talk on the phone about our days and it almost seems that a kind of friendship is emerging between us where the parent-as-disciplinarian relationship is becoming less necessary. I like it quite a lot actually. But perhaps that is because I still have the boys at home. This letter for Shawn's acceptance slammed me into a reality I had not thought of yet. That's not entirely true, I've thought of it, but I've thought of it from a distance thinking that I had loads of time left. I don't.

It's a curious thing really. It's kind of like the frenzy I work myself into the few days before Christmas. I know it's coming. I have 365 days to prepare for it every year and yet I let it happen because somehow, time has a way of fooling me into thinking I have plenty of time. With my children, I figured I had 18 years to prepare for their leaving home for college or wherever else their lives will take them when they leave our home to begin lives that are their own. I let this sneak up on me too. And though I am beginning a little earlier with my second child, I am already working myself into the next-to-the-last minute frenzy of letting go. But I also know that in September I will have Michael, my youngest still at home. I have plenty of time. He's only 12 after all; that gives me six years to get ready. Maybe I'd better start preparing now. ◉

Grampa's Car
KATHY KENNEY-MARSHALL

He'd waited 18 years to get his first car. A rite of passage I suppose, but this rite of passage was to be made sweeter because the car belonged to his grandfather. It wasn't a sports car, didn't have any fancy gadgets, bells or whistles, though the 14-year-old sun roof still worked. It was a Honda with 270,000 miles on it and the little red paper poppy, though faded and sad looking that his grandfather had put into the heating vent was still there. He got it from the war veteran's when he put a dollar in their collection box. That little flower reminded all of us of my father every time we sat in the car.

My dad died of esophageal cancer years ago and just one week later, my car conked out on Rt. 93 on my way home from writing thank you notes with his wife. I borrowed his car and knew as soon as I sat in it, that I had to have this car instead of buying a new one. It had 135,000 miles on it then, mere teenage-hood for any Honda as well taken care of as this one. It still had his white tic-tacs in the glove compartment, his cleaning rag that was always sprayed with Armor All under the seat, and that red poppy.

I drove it for a while, then we bought the mini-van that screamed, "soccer mom aboard" meaning I had to drive it. So my husband, Paul took over the Honda. But we knew that it would be Shawn's as soon he could drive. My older daughter drove my mom's hand-me-down, also a Honda, so the decision, though unspoken, sat in the back of my son's mind for years; he knew that he would get to have Grampa's car someday.

Fast forward several years and 135,000 more miles. Though I won't bore you the details of my daughter's bad luck with cars, I will tell you that Grampa's car was loaned to her for a short while until her brother was ready for it. We couldn't bear to see the car sitting idle in the driveway, so when circumstances arose that warranted the loan of the car, we gladly handed her the keys with the strict set of instructions about the use of this precious piece of Grampa.

But like people, cars die at one time or another. Nothing lasts forever. Ironically, it was on the way home to pick up her old car and hand the legacy over to her brother that the car took its last chug of fuel and died on the highway somewhere around W. Bridgewater. The mechanic called us with the bad news the next morning. It was gone, like my father. I found myself weepy again, missing my father. I felt like it was just yesterday that we sat down to watch one of the kids play in a baseball game and then realizing that he was not ever going to see one again.

When Paul went to clean out the car, I asked for the poppy that now sits between the pages of one of my journals with a note to him thanking him for letting us have a piece of him a little longer.

As my father was battling cancer, he always said, "When I beat this thing, I'm going to go out and buy myself a new Cadillac, and I'm paying cash. Life is too short to wait until tomorrow." So isn't it ironic that when I opened the paper the day after I placed that poppy in my journal, I saw an ad for a Cadillac, not new certainly, but a Cadillac nonetheless.

My son now has a car, only two weeks after Grampa's car went to Honda Heaven. We surprised him and brought him to see the 1991 black Caddy after already checking it out with the mechanic to make sure it was safe. Then we told him the story of his grandfather's lament about a Cadillac that spoke more about hope for a future than a car he didn't get a chance to have. So today Shawn drives his first car with the comfort of knowing that he really did get Grampa's car after all.

> *So isn't it ironic that when I opened the paper the day after I placed that poppy in my journal, I saw an ad for a Cadillac, not new certainly, but a Cadillac nonetheless.*

Hiding Things Where they Belong: A Lost Art Form.

KATHY KENNEY-MARSHALL

Remember Hide-and-Seek? When I was a child, I could have won an award for the being best hider in the neighborhood. Whether indoors or out, I could out-hide anyone. When we played indoors, I hid so well during a game when all of my older cousins were visiting, it was a good two hours before I was found. Or more accurately, before anyone actually noticed I was missing. I was hiding in the coat closet in the hallway behind my grandfather's huge overcoat. He found me. He wasn't even IT. He was leaving. After our weekly family pizza night he pulled his coat off the hanger and he found me sleeping wedged between the vacuum, my father's snow boots, and the carton of old tax returns. I wasn't old enough to feel bad about anything as petty as not being noticed, but I was annoyed that nobody, not even my parents saved me any pizza. What has dawned on me since is that being the youngest, I was not really the best hider, my older siblings and cousins had found a way to get me out of their hair without the punishments that usually followed their torment.

When I became a parent, it all came back to me because I could still hold the title for the Best Hider Award, if there is such a thing. It is not a title that I covet, but apparently I'm in the running nonetheless. My children search the internet regularly looking for ways to embarrass … ah … honor me with this designation. I hope I'm not alone in my latest parenting quandary.

Monday morning for example, my cell phone rang and I saw on my caller ID that one of my kids was calling. This couldn't be good at 7:09am. I wondered what the sibling quarrel was about this time. Of course, since I adore my children despite the arguments and cell phone calls that almost send me into roadside ditches, I answered the phone with a sweet , *"WHAT!?"* It was my youngest, Mike.

"Mom, what did you do with my bus pass?" was his question that, by the way, he was asking approximately 30 seconds before the bus was supposed to arrive.

"I haven't seen your bus pass" was my almost cheerful reply. I proceeded to list the several places he might find said bus pass, but kept the expletive suggestions, (have you checked up your _ _ _?) to myself. Though happy a melee over the last English muffin was not the reason for the call, I was just a little annoyed that I am always called upon to find any missing item in our home.

It seems that any time anything in the house is missing; it must be because "Mom hid it." For example, recently my daughter's cell phone was shut off because I hid her cell phone bills ... in the mail. I disguised them as cheerful little notes sent to her at her dorm. I first tried 'hiding' them in her bedroom ... on her pillow ... where I knew she would most certainly miss them when she came home on occasional weekends. When the overdue notice came, I decided my hiding place was clever, but not quite clever enough, so that's when I resorted to the US Postal Service. I sent the phone bills hidden inside the fold of a greeting card and wrote loving notes (Pay the bill or else!!! Love always, Mommy PS. How are you?), so she wouldn't be able to find those either. It worked. Apparently I've hidden them well enough since September and the cell phone company disconnected her. I'm getting as good at 'hide your children's stuff' as I was at hide-and-seek.

While making dinner recently, for example, my older son informed me that he "found" the Fruit Breezer cough drops I bought (and evidently hid). The fact that they were put away on the shelf with the cold medicines instead of thrown in the middle of the living room floor where they could be found easily meant I bought them to hide for my own depraved gratification.

I admit it, I like to hide things. I hide their socks in their laundry baskets, clean and folded. I hide their coats on hangers in the coat closet, and worst of all, I hide their CDs in the correct cases. I am a bad mother, but obviously I'm great at hiding anything of value to my family.

So, all you internet experts, I'm calling in a favor. Can you please do some research and let me know if there is such an award out there so I can try even harder to get my children to nominate me? I'm getting sloppy. The other day, I left my son's jacket and backpack right in the middle of the dining room where he left it. He had no trouble whatsoever finding it. Bad hider! But in my own defense, I left it there because after I tripped over it, I whacked my head against the dining room chair and rushed to the sink to make sure the light green carpet didn't get blood on it. I'm getting desperate. I need to find out where they can apply quickly because I'm obviously never going to be in the running for Mother of the Year and I need to earn some kind of trophy worth putting on the mantle!

Holiday Traditions are Worth Waiting for

KATHY KENNEY-MARSHALL

hen Paul and I approached our first Christmas as new parents, we brought with us holiday traditions from our respective families. For example, on that first Christmas Eve when our oldest daughter, Kalin, was only eight months old, we were very excited about Santa's first visit to our home. Not that Kalin would remember any of it, but we were determined it would be just as wonderful for her as it was for us when we were children. As I readied the brand new plate for Santa's cookies and opened the bag of carrots to leave out for the reindeer, I yelled to Paul to go the liquor store to get a six-pack of Miller Lite. He walked into the kitchen with a puzzled "you-don't-drink-beer-and-I- would-never-drink-LITE" look on his face. "Ahhh, you're in the mood for a beer?" he asked.

"*NO,* I don't drink beer, it's for Santa!" was my are-you-really-that stupid reply.

That was the first time I ever thought my husband might wet his pants as he laughed himself onto the floor. I, on the other hand was shocked. Didn't everyone leave a beer, (or six), for Santa Claus. Milk? I had never heard of such a thing. After Paul calmed down, we agreed that milk went with the cookies a little better and I even chuckled a bit.

As our family has grown and grown up, many traditions have become a part of our holiday. Of course, then there is the tradition of fighting over ... I mean, picking out the Christmas tree. Every year, we have a mandatory attendance policy for this very important ritual. We (argue) talk all the way to Stanney's, the local tree seller, and slam the doors to the mini-van as we embark on our hunt. Many happy families are strolling around looking at trees, to inspect for bald spots or to find the perfect top for a star. Our disagreement (melee) usually entails how wide or how tall the tree is, the shape, the color, and the needle appearance. I am the cause for the disharmony according to the children, while Paul simply follows us around, holding up trees for me to hate. In my own defense, my father and I, on the last Christmas I lived with him, sought out and bought the ugliest most pitiful tree on the lot, deciding that if we didn't buy it, it would end up in the landfill or worse as kindling in someone's fireplace. I figure I am owed a practically perfect tree for the rest of my life as my reward for saving that poor tree 21 years ago. We almost always end up buying the very first tree we looked at in the first place and by then, everyone is so foul tempered, we have to wait a few days to decorate it for fear of someone accidentally tipping it over (on me).

There are lots of other traditions as well. The Christmas card with the adorable picture of my kids, that each year my kids swear is the last, is still mailed. I find joy in writing messages to those I don't see often. I buy stickers to decorate the envelopes and hand-write every address even though my computer could easily generate labels. Paul bakes oatmeal raisin cookies for loads of his co-workers and I bake cinnamon vanilla coffee cakes for mine. Our youngest, Mike, refuses to listen to any Christmas music until Christmas Eve, an unusual tradition he started for himself several years ago. When he walks into a room where I am listening to this forbidden music, he runs from the room, hands over his ears screaming, *"LALALALA? I DON"T HEAR THAT!"* My daughter's custom, adhered to strictly is that she refuses to wrap a gift. On Christmas morning, after her own gifts are opened, she saunters into her room and hands each of us a bag from whichever store she bought our gift. I was a little nervous the year she handed me a Home Depot bag, but she had merely bought my gift at the same store as someone else's, so she used a Home Depot bag to distinguish mine. Whew!

Christmas Eves now consist of old traditions and new. We go to Fatima Shrine to stroll through and look at the lights. We light candles for those family members not still with us and pray for those who need it. Before we leave, we open the cookie dough ornaments; a fairly new tradition. I buy these people-shaped ornaments that most closely resemble each family member and they show what is going on for each that year. If you read my column about hiding my daughter's cell phone

> *I realized today as I drove home from the overcrowded mall, that I didn't think about the gift part of Christmas at all when I thought about traditions.*

Holiday Traditions are Worth Waiting for

bills, you won't be surprised to know that her ornament is a girl holding a cell phone with the words "NO SERVICE" across the screen. I'm sure she'll find it as funny as last year's ornament that had her car insurance bill that read CANCELLED across the paper the cookie dough teen held. We spend the evening with Paul's family eating dinner and recently have begun having a Yankee Re gift Swap. We take the most awful gifts we have received over the year, wrap them up, and re-gift. The only danger here is in remembering who gave that ugly gift. It's so much fun and we laugh until our sides ache.

    I realized today as I drove home from the overcrowded mall, that I didn't think about the gift part of Christmas at all when I thought about traditions. Sure, presents are fun, but the true joy of this holiday, for me anyway, lies in the rituals that bring us together as a family to laugh or even argue. I also realized that what I enjoy most of all is the same thing I loved as a child; the anticipation of Christmas customs. So as I sit here writing this column, I think about how we all used to say, "I can't wait for Christmas" and I know ... I love waiting.

A Little Hope Under the Tree
KATHY KENNEY-MARSHALL

My husband, Paul, and I have decided to make a change this holiday season. During the only time of the year when gifts are bought to excess, we have decided to cut way back on each other's Christmas gifts. Just a small token of appreciation and love will do. No, nobody lost a job and there was no huge unexpected bill. But we have had an unexpected change in our lives that made the extravagance of Christmas seem more than a little frivolous.

Just last week, I read Mike Barnicle's column about a friend whose son who took his own life. The story made me really sad for his parents, people I don't even know. I thought about my own 19 year old as well as my other two children and wondered how I could ever cope if one of them decided that life was too hard to "stay in the game". I'm not sure I could survive it. But another thought, one that has been on my mind since September, became even more important. I thought about another teen, this one only 16, who wanted to live, but didn't.

We have been lucky enough to belong to a "family" of close friends. There are six couples altogether and with all of the kids, our extended family numbered 30. That is, until September 12th. On that Saturday night, one of "our" kids went on her confirmation retreat and died. She had a headache, went to lie down, and an aneurysm robbed her of the rest of what promised to be a long and exciting life. It was sudden, shocking, and unbearably painful for her parents, her sisters, and to all of us who had watched her grow from an adorable curly haired baby to a poised talented young lady. The shock has not yet worn off, but the question of why now haunts every one of us as we watch our own children navigate through their formative years. Her immediate family will never be the same. And though the rest of us go to work and school, and generally live our lives as normally as before, we will also never be quite the same.

When tragedy like this strikes, it puts so many things in perspective. It makes those dirty socks on the floor a little less annoying and that rude driver a lot less important. You worry less about whether the dishes are washed and are more mindful about saying "I love you" to your children every day. You think about regret and become more cognizant of controlling impulsiveness that causes it because, truthfully, there are so many occasions in which regret is beyond our control.

Mike Barnicle's column ended with his feeling of regret for a "life lost so senselessly". Yes, Mike, that's the kind of regret we have no control over. Your son's friend, Greg wanted to die and my friend's daughter wanted to live. Yet did either have any more control over the tragic outcome of their young lives? I doubt it. And do we have any control at all about how we cope in the aftermath? I hope so.

So instead, I will work on what I can control and remember to show these people I love how much they count. Perhaps knowing that is one of the greatest gifts we can give.

The holidays bring these tragedies into an even sharper focus than any of us want them to be. So when I think about Christmas this year, the gift I want most of all is one I know I cannot have; the control to prevent these kinds of losses for any family, especially those with so much promise, like my chosen one. So instead, I will work on what I can control and remember to show these people I love how much they count. Perhaps knowing that is one of the greatest gifts we can give. But maybe what I can get a hold of this Christmas is a bit of hope. In hope, there is a future filled with possibility. I think we could all use a little right about now.

And even if we can't find it within ourselves at the moment ... well, "Santa? Are you listening?" ◉

Is Lying Just a Part of Growing Up?
KATHY KENNEY-MARSHALL

It starts young for most. In my case, I remember a gingham dress and a green crayon. I was watching cartoons absentmindedly rolling the unpapered crayon up and down the hem of the dress. During the commercial break of *Kimba the White Lion*, I looked down to continue my coloring book masterpiece. I could multi-task even at the age of five. But it was then I saw it ... the green crayon markings on my beautiful pink gingham. I panicked, ran to my mother, and confessed. Well, I almost confessed. What I really did was lie. I told her I must have gotten grass stains on it during kindergarten. My mother told me not to worry, it would come out in the wash. But the lie was heavy and I found that I couldn't hold it for more than a few minutes when I truly confessed, now to two crimes.

It's a part of growing up as most of us with children know. Kids try on lies like new clothes. They see how they fit and how comfortable or uncomfortable they are. Hopefully, with the proper response and lessons from parents the lies feel like itchy unlined wool pants that are two sizes too small. Then they can outgrow this stage and come to the realization that while the truth is often also uncomfortable, in the long run, it is a better choice.

One of my own children took a little longer to learn this lesson and at eight years old, he took to lying like a fish takes to water. The lies were numerous and foolish. Any question asked was a possible lie in the making. "Did you put away your bike?" "Yup". A glance out the window where the bike lay in the driveway exposed the lie. "Is your bed made?" "Did it this morning." A peek in the bedroom revealed another lie. "Mom! Mike stole my cookie." Mike was taking a nap. These lies weren't serious, but we know that the stakes get bigger as the kids do. I had to try something drastic since he was already grounded until he was 32. So I gave him a taste of his own medicine.

As I dropped him off at baseball practice, I promised him that when I picked him up, I would bring him to the new Wendy's in town. This was a real treat since I am not a fan of fast food. He nearly choked me with a thank you hug before getting out of the car. When pick up time came, I drove home. His question of "What are we doing here?" was promptly answered with innocence; "We live here, Silly." He reminded me quickly, "You said you would take me to Wendy's!". My clever response, made without malice as I got out of the car was, "I lied, how does it feel?" I left my eight year old son sitting in shocked silence. This is a rather unusual way to handle lying because I don't condone being untruthful, but I honestly thought that he might get the message if he was left with a strong example.

But as my children have grown older and I have hopefully grown wiser with experience, I have given the subject a lot of thought and these thoughts bring up important questions. Since it seems that everybody, adults and kids alike, tell untruths I often wonder; what prompts the telling of falsehoods? Is it in fact a developmental stage in the growing up process, or in the case of perjuring parents, a stage that is never outgrown? And if that's the explanation, have we just gotten really good at it as a society? And more importantly, is it ever ok to lie?

I haven't come up with the answers to these questions and neither have the psychologists who are paid abundantly to study the phenomenon of "being economical with the truth". The names for it are numerous and the scholars can call it what they want, I still call it lying.

So while I haven't come up with earth shattering answers I think, perhaps, that there are times when it's ok to fib a little. For example to save someone's feelings from being hurt, a little stretch of the truth may be warranted. You know, if the perm someone got leaves them looking like a French poodle, or the dress they bought brings out their worst features, then, I think it's not only ok, but it's kind to find something nice to say. But on the other end of the spectrum, it is never alright to hurt someone you love by being dishonest. Not ever.

As I try to teach my own kids and the kids in my classroom this very simple but non-negotiable rule, I sometimes find myself fighting a noble cause but a losing battle. I won't give up though, because in the end we do have to face ourselves every day. And when I look in the mirror, I can call myself many things, but liar is not one of them. For that I am thankful. ◉

Learning How to Train Your Child

KATHY KENNEY-MARSHALL

I subscribe to the notion that our journey through life should be full of learning experiences. When we graduate from high school or college, the learning shouldn't stop. Though we go through stages when we think we know everything, all one needs to do is to have children to once again realize how little we know.

But as I said, since the learning should never stop we pick up tidbits of knowledge and hopefully we are able to figure things out by trial and error. Never mind the parenting books. While you might be able to gather smidgens of book smarts, the real life stuff is what I personally have gleaned the most information from. And being a generous person by nature, I've decided to share a few lessons with my fellow parents in whose children's eyes, know nothing. And pay attention future dummy moms and dads so you too can claim to know one or two things that your kids don't:

1.) It's ok to lie to children as long as you are doing it for health reasons. My children thought the truck that came only in the summer playing annoyingly happy music was driven by the fish man for years. They thought it was gross that all those neighborhood kids lined up in the heat for a piece of yucky haddock.

2.) It's also ok to lie to teach a lesson; like, don't lie. When one of my children was eight years old, he lied for the fun of lying. He wouldn't lie about anything important and he often lied in a way that was not even smart. "Did you make your bed?" "Yes" "I'm going to check." "Fine." Of course the bed was not made. We tried everything. Nothing worked. We were desperate. So one day when he had baseball practice, I promised to bring him to Wendy's when I picked him up. After practice I drove home. He asked, "Why are we here, you promised to take me to Wendy's." My answer? "I lied, how does it feel?" I don't usually condone "an eye for an eye" but when all else fails, it's fine to resort to desperate measures.

3.) You can get your kids to eat almost anything with the proper motivation. On Halloween for example, serve something totally nutritious that you've been dying to get your kids to eat like, Lentil Loaf. YUM! Make it a condition of their ability to go trick-or-treating. It's a little sadistic fun for us and we get them bulked up on health food before they go to penny candy purgatory.

4.) There is no sure fire way to clear your teenage kids out of a room than talking about something completely uncomfortable. Especially if they are boys who have friends visiting. If they are blasting obnoxiously loud video games, and you want to watch a chick flick all you must do is bring up the topic of sex in the guise of a how-to lecture. I told them I had seen a parenting documentary on rising teen pregnancy that suggested bringing home a condom in order to show your teen boys how to use it. My subsequent question of "Do you need me to do that?" had them running out of the room so fast they left trail marks in the carpet. The movie was terrific.

5.) If you want to know what's going on in your teen's life, offer to chauffeur as often as possible. Grunt hello calling as little attention to yourself as possible and then shut up and listen. They often forget you're there and you hear all sorts of valuable information. I am fascinated by the more important gossip, like who is dating who, who is grounded and for what, and most importantly, who is that new hot teacher who's covering a maternity leave. I can't wait for the next Open House to meet Mr. _____.

6.) Going through your kids things while they aren't home is perfectly legal as long as you do it under the guise of "I-was-looking-for-your-favorite-left-gym-sock-with-the-lucky-hole," or my personal favorite, "I-know-I-saw-your-brother's-tarantula -run-in-here-and-thought-it-might-be-hiding-between-the-pages-of-your-diary." Of course, this one only works if your son does in fact have a tarantula. Be flexible with your alibi.

By this time you must be thinking, "Wow! She knows everything about raising kids! They must be so well trained ... (I mean behaved)!" I would agree except the other night, my older son used a knife to cut pepperoni and cheese. He then proceeded to put the knife back in its butcher-block slot claiming he was sure that since the new Ronco knives I bought were so expensive, they had to be self-cleaning. Wise guy. He still has a lot to learn. Apparently, so do I. When I figure out how to teach, aka, manipulate him into washing every dirty dish in the house, I'll let you know. ◉

Fumble or Touchdown?
KATHY KENNEY-MARSHALL

I ate lunch with a friend the other day in a rare moment void of the chaos that follows working parents. Over a salad and a chilled glass of chardonnay, we pondered the tumult of high school football. Both of us have sons who play. We were lamenting both the laundering of dirty practice uniforms after rainy three-to-four hour practices as well as the intolerable hour that said practices ended each evening.

I had an epiphany that day that boggles my mind. We spend 16 years teaching our kids ways to keep safe. From the time they are babies we are teaching them about the dangers they will inevitably face. Don't talk to strangers we tell them. Look both ways before you cross the street. Hold my hand in the store. Buckle your seatbelt. We teach them not to run on the stairs, not to touch a hot stove, and not to put anything into an electric socket. As they get older, the lessons don't end, they just become more important and certainly scarier to parents. Don't do drugs. Don't walk the streets at night alone. Don't drink and drive and don't get into cars with anyone else who has been drinking. Safety. It's what we do as parents. And then without thought, we send them onto a football field to maim, incapacitate, or demolish the guy with the ball. They break legs, arms, and crack skulls. Cartilage is torn, tendons ruptured, and bodies are bloodied, all in the name of a high school game. And we watch this violence, cheering them on and encouraging them to rest up for the next torture session.

To make matters even more curious, we leave them under the supervision of a grown man whose sole purpose it is to unleash his frustration over never having made the NFL himself. He is as inflexible as a steel rod and flaunts his self-imposed power as if the outcome of a holocaust depended on it. I exaggerate, but only slightly. I have come to believe that if you looked up *football coach* in a thesaurus, 'tyrant' might appear as one of the synonyms. I often wonder why football coaches in real life can't be like the ones in the movies. You know, like Ed Harris's portrayal of Coach Jones, a tough yet fair-minded man with the capacity for compassion in *Radio*. Or Denzel Washington in *Remember the Titans*. He actually cried in a rare glimpse of football coach human emotion. In real life, the kids barely tolerate him and the parents have anxiety attacks every time their sons are approached during a game fearing that this time, the tyrant's tantrum might be unleashed on their offspring.

So why do we let them do it? Why do we let them put themselves at the mercy of a heartless coach and in the line of 200 pound body crunchers day after day, week after week? I don't believe it is simply for the love of the testosterone driven brutality that makes them male. I believe it is for the togetherness that makes them a group separate from us. No matter how our parental hackles rise with each temper tantrum the coach throws if they make a mistake, don't run fast enough, or fumble, they are willing to deal with it without us. No matter how we long to run out on that field to 'fix' each bruise and bump, we can't. They have set their own boundary that protects them from our nurturing. They face what looks like misery to us, but they are in this misery together and as we all know, misery loves company.

Which makes my son's decision to leave the team last week surprising. He had been training for his senior year on the football team since school ended last June. He lifted weights, ran miles and miles, attended the mandatory camp in August, and started the season on schedule. His phone call that afternoon took me off guard. He told me how he went to the coach to talk. He explained with wisdom far older than his years that he was not motivated by the daily beratings of himself and his teamates. He explained that while he understood how some players tolerate his method of coaching, he was not energized by it. He recognized that this was the root of his yearly autumn anxiety that caused unhappiness that was spilling over into every other aspect of his life. So he did what was right for him and left the team. The coach's response didn't surprise me. He said, "it's easy to quit when things get tough". Obviously this coach isn't half the man that my son is. This was one of the hardest decisions he has ever had to make in his young life. He dealt with being called a quitter by the coach with integrity and answered the barrage of questions from classmates. He didn't quit, he left the team with the realization that he was giving up a lot. He cast aside a poor role model and instead made choices that were productive. A quitter doesn't think things out thoroughly and make healthy mature decisions. A quitter doesn't face obstacles head on and have difficult discussions with people who will never see their side. It was a tough decision, but for him, the right one despite the loss of the team and the love of the game. I can honestly say, I've never been more proud of my son. ◉

Christmas Memories Last Longer Than a Day

KATHY KENNEY-MARSHALL

Christmas may be over but the memories that are made each year ought to last past New Year's Eve. So I thought I'd share a few thoughts about this year's Christmas with the old traditions that I wrote about a short while ago and make an observance or two about a few new ones.

On Christmas Eve, Paul, Mike, and I took our annual trip to the Fatima Shrine. We missed last year because of the rain that was falling sideways in gusts that would surely blow me over into one of the light displays. We have umbrellas here, but even with the six inches of umbrella coverage, the rain threatened to ruin a perfect hair day for me, a sacrifice I was not willing to make even for tradition. I know that may seem shallow, but my husband's family, with whom we spend Christmas Eve, is a group of exceptionally good looking people and I could not spend the night looking like a drowned rat. But in missing our trip last year, we missed a few changes or rather additions that had been made at the Shrine. For example, we must have missed the red, green, blue, and yellow lights of the new choo-choo train that blinks, waves, and could possibly blind you if you aren't wearing sunglasses in the dark of night. We must have missed the unveiling of the other equally unreligious exhibits of toys and symbols that were added. We also noticed that the singing of, *It's Beginning To Look A Lot Like Christmas* replaced the somber, holy choir music being piped in over the loudspeakers throughout the walk around the Stations of the Cross. Sure, the crèche is still there, but instead of quietly saying prayers as we stood around it, we watched young children, bundled in their winter clothes chucking pennies at the baby Jesus screaming, *"I GOT"M! Did'ja see that Dad?"* Luckily, we were able to find the candle stall free of mayhem and we lit candles for people who were not joining us for Christmas this year. We sadly lit candles and prayed for our fathers, both Paul and mine, who we lost to cancer, for Great Grandmother, who at 102, left her mark indelibly etched in our hearts, for Uncle Eddie who recently passed away, and for

Sara, our dear friend's daughter who died only three months ago. As we walked away in quiet thought, we were almost knocked down by a brother and sister who thought this the perfect setting for a jaunty game of tag. Thank goodness for their raucous laughter jolting us out of memories. As we finally made our way to a quieter area, it was rather nice to walk alone with our youngest son for whom this tradition is most important. He is the one who reminds us that we need to go if we get too caught up in the preparations of the holiday. He thinks he may bring his own children here when he grows up and becomes a dad. You never know what they will take with them, do you?

All the way to Paul's niece's home in Holliston, we began a new tradition. We judged/rated the decorations on houses that tried to display the spirit of Christmas. All I have to say is that the understated simplicity of white lights, window candles, and door wreaths won over those houses whose owners simply threw up whatever they found on sale during the after holiday sales last year leaving their displays looking like ... well, throw up!

> *We had our hilarious Yankee Regift Swap, where the gifts are funny and the swapping even funnier.*

When we arrived at Missy and Brian's house who are due with their first child in April, we all took turns touching her emerging belly beginning the Pillsbury Dough-boy tradition for further nieces who happen to be pregnant on Christmas Eve. We had our hilarious Yankee Regift Swap, where the gifts are funny and the swapping even funnier. Apparently watching grown people snatch a relative's favorite gift of plastic pink flamingoes is tons of fun.

The next morning, as the kids woke and were allowed in the living room where Santa unloaded his gifts, they were blessed (or cursed?) with this year's entertaining mechanical creature (my contribution, I admit it). This year's amusement? A song from "Mr White Christmas", a dancing, singing, hat tipping, tinsel swinging homosexual snowman. The pictures of their stunned faces are priceless. They can hardly wait to see what kind of oddity shows up next year. But the most amazing change in tradition for our family? Kalin actually wrapped our Christmas gifts! No more Home Depot bags for Mom, no CVS bag for Dad, and no price tags left on the gifts to let

Christmas Memories Last Longer Than a Day

us know exactly how much we mean to her ($1.75 comes to mind for some reason, but perhaps that was several years ago). She said that she wanted to show us all that she really did want to give something meaningful, and by meaningful she meant taking her time and making these gifts look nice for us. What lay inside mattered less, but were thoughtful just the same. I was truly touched. It only took 19 years, but we received the best gift of all; the sacred time a teenage child takes to be thoughtful. A new tradition? I hope so. But if not, I have the pictures to prove it happened.

The rest of the day was filled with old traditions that we look forward to every year. We have friends over for brunch then head up to New Hampshire to stay over at my mother's for a great afternoon of laughter, food, and terrific company. The gifts are fun, but not as important as the memories we are creating for a lifetime. ◉

Picking Favorites

KATHY KENNEY-MARSHALL

Once upon a time I was the favorite child in my family. It lasted approximately three and a half minutes. I won't bore you with the details, but I bring it up because my son is writing his college essay and decided to write about the curse of being the middle child. At first I was horrified. How could he call his position cursed? As it turns out, his essay made the assertion that this curse had not in fact been inflicted upon him. He believed that my husband and I raised all three of our children in a fair and equal way. Whew. This brings up an interesting parenting question though: is it ever ok to have a favorite? I think we would be lying if we said no. I'm guilty of having a favorite child. There, I said it. So I did a little inquisition and this is how it came out.

I was driving with Shawn, 17, and asked "the question". He remarked that my daughter, 19, was without a doubt my favorite. My mouth dropped open in shock. I immediately thought about the unkind and angry remarks that escaped my mouth just the day before. I believe the phrase I used had something to do with "having a major, (insert a swear word here rhyming with witch) issue she'd better deal with before she went off to college to live with someone who didn't love her like I did". A loving statement if ever I heard one. I too, say things in exasperation in the heat an unpleasant moment. And while it's true, she does need to learn to tone it down; my words might have been better accepted if stated differently. My favorite? Hmm, I'm not sure that honor would have belonged to her on that day. But when she took her youngest brother to the movies because he was bored and I was busy and she didn't want to see a full- length feature cartoon, she was my favorite. And when she sat on the couch after skipping school and sobbed because her best friend had gotten pregnant and she didn't know how to face her or what to say, my heart ached for her and swelled with favorite child love. So maybe, Shawn had a point. Of course,

Picking Favorites

when I asked Kalin the "favorite child" question, she answered that Michael, 12, is my favorite. A questionable answer in that Michael is quickly becoming his own worst enemy ... and quite possibly mine. What comes to mind quickly is the shattered door wreath with its beautiful red and white berries crumbled into the grout on the newly tiled entry. I am struck by the dirty socks left in a trail wherever he decides his feet are too hot, or the dead fish in an aquarium that hasn't been cared for. My favorite? I'm not sure those actions scream favoritism. But, when I think of that morning after a wrist surgery, when Michael made me raisin toast and brought it up to my bed. He reheated coffee from the day before; loaded it with sugar and so much cream it was barely warm. He burned the toast a bit and barely buttered it. It was quite awful really, but the look of love in his eyes made it the most remarkable breakfast I ever had. Right at that moment, he was my favorite. And when he snuggled up close to me, not caring that big boys don't cuddle with their mothers, I thought for sure, this is my favorite child.

But when I asked Michael "the question" his emphatic answer was that Shawn is my favorite. In Michael's eyes, Shawn can stay up as late as he wants and gets to boss him around. To the youngest boy, the oldest boy must certainly be the favorite. But is he? I was searching for the phone recently and asked for help finding it. Shawn answered, "Why should I look, you're the one who needs it." Although kidding, I did not find his disrespectful jab humorous at all. My favorite child would never speak to me that way. My favorite would also never ever call me on my cell phone to report how my daughter was being an a** ... yes, an a**. If I ever said a** in front of my mother at 17, I would have been slapped. My favorite child would also never berate me for being so cheap that I would *only* cough up $60 for sneakers to wear to the gym. No, a favorite child would not do this. But how do those things compare to him making me laugh almost every day of my life? When I am at my lowest, busiest, most anxious, Shawn says something to make me laugh. One night I had too much to do after work and he needed a ride to CCD. CCD was *NOT* in my plans for the night. I was stressed out and not feeling very rational. He stood in front of me, hands in the air screaming with drama, " But Mom! I need a little Jesus!" I stopped and collapsed into laughter and somehow, my night went a whole lot better. He was my favorite that night. And my most cherished moment was when he sat next to me in church during my father's first anniversary Mass. As I sat staring at my own knees to keep from crying, I felt his hand extend to mine and he held onto me for the rest of the service. Most certainly, he was my favorite then.

So here it is; I have favorites. I am not ashamed of it and will easily admit it if asked. I suppose it just depends on what day it is. It depends on the ebb and flow of the every day stuff life is made of. It may depend on what we are able to give to and receive from each other. As they become older, I find that I like so much about each one. Shawn's sense of humor and sensitivity make him my favorite. Kalin's energy and intensity make her my favorite. Michael's compassion and eagerness to please make him my favorite.

> *How lucky I am really to have learned in my life, that not only is it ok to have a favorite, I am fortunate enough to have three. I could not ask for more than that.*

How lucky I am really to have learned in my life, that not only is it okay to have a favorite, but I am fortunate enough to have three. I could not ask for more than that. ⊙

Pretty in the City or Slacker Mom?
KATHY KENNEY-MARSHALL

While reading a *MWD* column the other day, I was intrigued by an invitation at the end of the column to take an online quiz that would tell me for certain what kind of mother I am. Anyone who has read my column for any length of time knows my obsession with becoming some sort of unearthly Super Mom, so I had to take the quiz. I thought about and answered each question carefully because I realized the gravity of this test. The name alone was daunting; "Are you a slacker mom?" I poured myself a hearty glass of wine and began.

Question 1.) Are you a mom or a dad? This was a straightforward question. I am definitely a mom.

Question 2.) What age are you? Hmmm, is this a trick? Is it better to be older or younger? Never mind, just answer truthfully; 40-45 was my category (and that's all you need to know).

Question 3.) How many children are you lucky enough to have? Are they kidding? Lucky? That is definitely a matter of opinion depending on what day you ask me ... or what time of day. I have three children.

Question 4.) How old your cherubs (yes, they actually used that word, and I don't remember thinking of them as "cherubs" since they were under one and were sleeping). Check all that apply they instructed. I had to check three categories to cover my 20, 18, and 13 year olds. By the way, what difference does it make how old my "cherubs" are when determining Mother Sainthood?

Question 5.) What is a typical lunch for my children? 'Foul, foul, no fair' was my immediate thought. I cannot compete with those yummy fish sticks and those fruit cups sweetened with high fructose corn syrup that the school cafeteria offers as opposed to the peanut butter and mayonnaise sandwiches on multi-grain-hard-as-a-rock bread that I would be glad to make at home. Well, there are other questions I'm sure.

Question 6.) What is your schooling? Yes! Finally a Mother-of-the-Year question: Master's Degree, HA!

Question 7.) What is your profession other than Mom? These choices were harder but I finally chose, full-time Mom, full-time work.

Question 8.) What is your "other" job? The choices here were difficult again. I chose "stand and deliver" because as a teacher, I stand up a lot and deliver lessons.

Question 9.) What is my favorite way to 'de-stress'? Check all that apply. This is tricky ... it's anonymous right? I power shop, aka, retail therapy, go to the gym, go for a girls' night out, or lose myself in a book. A well rounded answer if I do say so myself.

Question 10.) What was the last TV show I watched from start to finish? No hesitation, *Sex in the City*. Were they kidding with the *MacNeil/Lehrer Report*?

Question 11). Uh-oh. What is my debt level? Since "none of your damn business" was not an option, I decided to be honest; "don't get me nervous, where does all that money go?" This is a tough test ... I need more chardonnay.

Question 12.) Do you own your own home? Yippee! An easy one. Yes!

Question 13.) Do you have pets? Another easy one; no, (does a husband count?)

Question 14.) What is your marital status? Duh, I just answered that in question 13.

Question 15.) Phew, almost done. What family activities do you participate in? Excellent question; we travel (does the mall the next town over count?), movies, sports, and other, (other meaning fighting over the bathroom.)

Finally finished, I clicked the "submit" button and eagerly awaited the results which came in under three seconds. Apparently, I am a "Pretty in the City Mom". Huh ... way better than Slacker Mom! I reported my results, (18 times) to my family until they finally told me

Pretty in the City or Slacker Mom?

to stop. Then, being a good journalist, I decided to take the test several more times without such honesty to see what other kinds of moms there are in the world. After taking the test two more times, I came out as a "Bring It On Mom, and a Smarty Pants Mom". I got suspicious. Since the only good answer I gave on the "Smarty Pants Mom" quiz was that I had a PHD, I took the test one more time and gave answers that I deemed the worst choices of each question. I had myself quitting school at age 10, had no significant other but 12 "cherubs", I had no "other" job and I didn't feed my kids daily. But I did go out with my friends to de-stress, along with overindulging in chocolate, wine, and cigarettes. What kind of mom did that make me according to the survey? These answers made me a "Pretty in the City Mom".

    I think, perhaps, these online quizzes may not be the best judge of my excellence as a mother ... I hope. ◉

Reality in Reality Television
KATHY KENNEY-MARSHALL

I have an idea for a new television reality show. I'm sure I'll make a fortune and I don't really have to do much work. Actually, I'll have to do a lot of work, so I should more accurately say, I won't have to do any *more* work than I already do. I even have a name for my new show; *"The Invisible Mother."* It will be great, or at least, it will make mothers all over the nation realize that they are not alone. An incredible support group will emerge almost instantaneously when the first show airs ... opposite SURVIVOR, (Please forgive me Jeff Probst, god-like human being that you are with dimples that ... never mind).

Anyway, I can imagine my pitch to whatever network wins the corporate battle to own my show for the first season it airs, (and then the subsequent 8 years until my youngest turns 21). Not unlike Jerry Seinfeld, I will pitch my show in the simplicity of real life, though my show will *NOT* be about nothing, it will be about the *THE* nothingness of motherhood. It will be a show about how absolutely ignorant the offspring we spawn think us to be. I'm already thinking about my first episode.

Fade into an immaculate (translation, cluttered embarrassment) living room on a Sunday night where the mother (me) played by ... Angelina Jolie, (is there anyone else?) is frantically cleaning up so the cleaning woman can clean on Monday morning. The laundry piles are high, but separated according to family member ownership. As Angelina rips in a hurry through the room, she pleasantly asks for the two children who are sprawled across the newly vacuumed micro-fiber sofas to make sure that their respective piles are put away by morning. There is no response of course because as we real mothers know, it takes at least three attempts at communication with offspring to attain any form of detection. She stops momentarily, raising the volume of her voice to match that of *The Simpsons* episode that has them mesmerized. No luck. Finally, she stands in front of the 72 inch plasma television and bellows, "Will someone please acknowledge that I spoke?!" A flicker of recognition crosses their faces as the oldest, moves her head ever so slightly to see Homer eat the family goldfish, while the younger with a smaller head responds with a barely intelligible, "huh?" His eye level has not moved making her diamond studded naval ring, showing slightly under a clingy black tank top that all real mothers wear to clean, appear fascinating. Though the thought is a bit revolting, we must not forget, he is still trying to see *The Simpsons,* not his gorgeous mother's naval.

The husband, who is playing computer cribbage in the next room offers support ... to the children by laughing at her comment and adding, "can you ask the bigger one to finish in the kitchen?" Angelina, shakes her head, laughing ever so slightly and replies, "of course dear" to which he calls out, *"WHAT?* I can't hear you over Bart and Lisa." The invisible mother then pours herself a hefty glass of chardonnay and disappears, babbling incoherently to herself as she drags herself and all of the laundry up the stairs, the wine precariously balanced on the top of the laundry basket. Men all over the country will watch for the occasional glimpse of the belly ring, while women, though hating the fact that Invisible Mom is always perfectly made up and has a stomach flatter than they had when they were 12, will still be able to get beyond that for the undertone that will carry this show; it is the tedious unrecognized chores of motherhood that get our families through their lives without them ever realizing what we do. The dirty glasses left in the living room are not picked up by the glass fairies and the dirty socks are not put in the laundry by the dirty sock gnomes. Usually it is the Invisible Mother, (and to be fair, in some homes, Brad Pitt plays the Invisible Father).

But the series does have one major flaw that has nothing to do with laundry or short shirts. The Invisible Mother will actually be visible ... once the children need a ride to the mall. Hmmmm ... it's a problem, I know, but I am still working out the kinks. ☉

> *Not unlike Jerry Seinfeld, I will pitch my show in the simplicity of real life, though my show will* NOT *be about nothing, it will be about* THE *nothingness of motherhood.*

The Pain and Pride of Leaving Home

KATHY KENNEY-MARSHALL

hough I've often written about the varying stages of my children's lives they do forgive me most of the time. But there is a stage in child development I found myself completely unprepared for; the day they leave.

I tried to shake off my sad feelings as silly because this is a good thing, surely the way it's supposed to be. It's the day your child moves out of home; not for college and not because of a nasty parent/child argument when you know they will return when they are hungry, but because they want to spread their wings and try life on their own.

It's why we have children isn't it? We want to create a family and teach our children how to be good people. We go through all the stages of childhood, the good and the awful. And all in all, when we sit down as a family for a meal or just to watch television, I have found myself almost always exactly where I want to be.

The growing up is inevitable. I knew it before, I know it now, and yet, I am sad that it has come.

My daughter, Kalin will be 21 soon. She took a semester off from college to work and though Paul and I thought that this would be a good time for self-reflection and saving, it seemed to be nothing more than a free ride at home with a job as a waitress in Boston. She enjoyed her job waiting on tables, delivering drinks, munchies, and meals of burgers and salads. We started charging her rent because that's what grown-ups do ... they pay for their room and board. She had it made, (although she still never made her bed.)

So the morning she came to the bathroom door and said, "Mom, I'm going to move out." I dropped my hairdryer and just stared. The questions were bumping into each other in my head, yet none of them made it to my mouth so she spoke. She was asked to join three other young women to live in an apartment in South Boston; Southie to the locals.

"It'll be great, Mom. You can visit and we'll go to Castle Island. I'm right down the street! I'll have my own room and my share of the rent is only $350!"

There was a sparkle in her eyes and an excited determination in her voice that I hadn't heard from her before. I didn't know how to react or what to say so I said the practical (stupid) mother thing: "You can't afford it."

"This will make me more responsible, Mom. It's time."
And with those words hanging between us, I forced back the tears that were threatening to fall and tried to smile. My daughter wanted to grow up and take care of herself. Isn't that what this parent thing is all about anyway? I should have felt a swelling of pride, and I did ... sort of. It's just that I would miss her. I would miss her smile, I would miss her company, I would just miss her.

I know Southie is not far, but it is not home. But she was right. It was time; time because she felt it was time and it doesn't really matter whether I did. It's time because as an almost-21-year-old, she should be experiencing what life has to offer outside of the umbrella of her parents.

She asked me the day she left, "Mom, let me put eye make-up on you." I didn't really want to, but I sat and let her do her thing. She carefully worked on my eyelids and we had a great mother/daughter moment. When I looked, (and I'm still not sure I loved it), I almost ruined her eye-art by crying as I thought, "who will I do this with now?" When she was small, I remember the awful hairdos she imposed on me. You know the kind with 85 pink and purple barrettes? I'm not sure I appreciated those times like I should have. Maybe this eye makeup gave me great hindsight.

As I watched her drive away from our home to her new one, I did in fact ruin my new eyes with tears of emotion. I was sad, yes, but more than anything, the single thought in my head, not bumping into anything else was;

"I wonder if Paul can make her room into a walk-in closet."

The Breast-feeding Debate Lives On
KATHY KENNEY-MARSHALL

I had lunch with friends, who are at different stages of mother development. I know that most of us think about child development when we have kids, but I continue to develop and learn as do all mothers right along with our kids. Two of my friends brought along their babies, 10-month-old Grace and 13-month-old Luke. I remembered when my babies were their age. They depended on me for everything and survived despite it.

We got to talking about important mothering issues and though the topic of cloth vs. disposable diapers provided some mild entertainment for the three of us who are out of that stage, the real story of the afternoon became the breast vs. the bottle debate that apparently has heated up even more than when I had babies. I remember being pregnant with my first child. I didn't give the idea much thought until the day my male boss asked me if I was going to bottle feed or starve my child. Today we would call that harassment, back then it was a "joke", albeit unfunny to me. This is yet another way the world has changed for the better. No one would dare say that to a woman today.

The new moms enlightened me with worlds of information on how the conflict has changed since I lost touch. That happened when I stopped reading parenting magazines because I had finally mastered the art of being a practically perfect parent ... or perhaps it was because my kids got too old for the content of the magazines.

One argument is no longer about whether or not to breast feed, it's how long you should breast feed. One friend had begun the weaning process at seven months, while the other was still, she confessed, a "closet nurser" because her baby is over a year. Apparently there are rigid guidelines to adhere to that were not in place when I was at that stage of development in motherhood. The conservative side of the debate dictates that 12 months is when you should stop. Not only that, you should just pick an arbitrary day and stop cold turkey.

The more liberal side allows for longer breast feeding and suggests weaning slowly. But it also recommends that you don't tell anyone for fear of chastisement.

Another friend at lunch that day offered another closet breast feeding confession. She was not comfortable with the idea with her first child and several years later when in the hospital with her second, she decided to give it a try. Still feeling uncomfortable with the idea, she floundered at each attempt and according to the nurse, she didn't appear to be enjoying this part of being a new mother. Then the nurse questioned her reasons for breast feeding. My friend's very honest answer was that she heard she could lose weight if she did. I had to chuckle because I'm sure she's not the only one with that motivation in mind, but I'm also sure she's one of the few who had the courage to admit it in a maternity ward during a time of such hot debate on the topic. She decided to bottle feed when the nurse explained that her reason was one of the worst she had heard in her 789 years of nursing. I'm guessing compassion was not one of her finest qualities.

> *I remember being pregnant with my first child. I didn't give the idea much thought until the day my male boss asked me if I was going to bottle feed or starve my child.*

This question was raised by one mother whose children are even older than mine; "so when is it that babies are too old?"

"When they can ask for a brownie" came to mind immediately. What I said out loud however was it wasn't anybody's business but theirs when it came to this very personal decision. Sure, we've all read the studies that speak of the health advantages, but breast feeding isn't for everyone. I know moms who breast fed babies and those who didn't whose babies were equally healthy. The bottom line is that a mother should be able to decide what is best for her baby and for her. It shouldn't be up to anyone else. And for those who don't agree with that choice, I think the old adage is right on the money: "If I want your opinion, I'll tell you what it is."

And to that jerky boss I had, just for the record, I did not bottle feed and not one of my children starved. ◉

When Crime Hits Home

KATHY KENNEY-MARSHALL

I consider myself to be a fairly calm person most of time. I go to work, write, raise my family and generally am considered reasonable and accepting of the bumps in life's road. Which is why recently, I shocked myself with frightening feelings, and I felt on the verge of a temper tantrum of powerful proportions. It was an emotion that didn't fit me very well, though I found that I didn't want to let go of it too quickly. So I went looking for a way to unleash the animal beneath the calm looking exterior that I found staring back at me from the rearview mirror of my car. To make this more curious, this mortal madness stemmed from a kid's bicycle; but it was MY kid's bicycle.

While at the mall for a quick last minute birthday gift for my daughter, my cell phone rang, and on the other end was Mike. He was very upset to report that while at the park with his friends, someone had stolen his bike. There were witnesses who reported two teens were whacking away at his "ultra safe very expensive" bike lock with a hammer and a baseball bat. Their tools worked and off they rode before Mike's game of tag in the large wooden playground was finished.

I left the mall immediately and found myself seething in rage and protectiveness only found in the wild when a predator approaches a young tiger cub. I drove the streets of my town looking for teenagers on bikes not thinking at first about what I would do if I found the boys who surely would be much taller than I and certainly outweigh me by the amount of a small child. What would I be able to do? Use my third grade teacher scary look? Threaten with a time-out? My trade secrets as a teacher and a mother of younger children would do me no good here in the wilds of growing teens and crime. When that realization hit me, I felt hopeless about being able to protect my child against his own natural predators. In the wild, there would be a fight to the death. A mother lioness always wins. But here in suburbia, what would happen to me? I turned my car toward home feeling the pain of reality; I had already lost my ability to thwart the evils that Michael, at only 12 years, would begin to face.

In the end, the bike was returned in a "clandestine" meeting right on my front porch. An urgent knock on the door found a very nervous 15 year old, eyes darting up and down the street, explaining that he knew who stole the bike. He apparently felt bad for Mike and stole it back from the original thief. Whether he was telling the truth, covering up for himself, or was suffering an attack of conscience mattered not at the moment. I invited him in, gave him a cold drink, and a ten-dollar bill for his honesty. As he left, he insisted "I was never here, but you might want to call the police after I go." I felt myself embroiled in an inner dilemma: when the police came, I wanted to press charges, but in doing so, I would have to give up the name of the boy who returned the bike. I gave him my word and on that I had to remain faithful. But if I didn't tell his name, nothing would happen to the boy who stole the bike. The accused already has a record at the ripe old age of 15. I decided not to tell, so the 15-year-old delinquent walks the streets another day equipped with a hammer and a baseball bat, the tools of his trade, seeking out other kids' bikes to be stolen, stripped, and sold.

Mike is happy to have his bike and wants me to leave it alone. This is how it goes, he explains to me. At the playground, things have a way of working out. He's angry about the situation, but is willing to let sleeping dogs (delinquents) lie. I realize I may have to defer to the judgment of kids who know their own playground standards and codes of behavior. When we were young, it was more about playing fair and not cheating. Today, it seems more about crime, punishment, and street justice; places where mothers are not supposed to have a role beyond a certain age. It's not right, I know.

So given the lessons that can be learned here about loyalty and sticking up for a playground friend, I suppose this mother lioness will just lay low and become ever-more watchful in the future. But make no mistake, I will be the first to bare my teeth and strike if I ever witness this deviant behavior toward my child.

So predators, bigger than me or not, watch out ... nobody on earth is as strong as a mother when protecting her child. But it also leaves me feeling sad, as I learn that childhood ends far too early. ◉

Getting through the Teenage Years
KATHY KENNEY-MARSHALL

As our children get older, the problems of their babyhood become less traumatic. The winters of walking a croupy baby up and down the street are gone. The drool of teething exists only on the stained favorite sweater you saved for nostalgia's sake. The faded pictures from first and second grade with the spaces from lost baby teeth lay in an album waiting for the perfect time to give their childhoods back in a neat little box.

My children are now 20, 19, and 13, and thus far, adolescence is undoubtedly the toughest time. Though I still have one going through this awkward time of teenage trauma, I am often thankful that so far, we've all made it through in one piece.

We were lucky because our kids didn't get into much trouble. And though we weren't always able to laugh, there were times when as soon as they walked up to bedroom banishment, we would cover our faces with the sofa pillows and belly laugh.

Shawn's skipping half a day of school comes to mind. He was a sophomore on the baseball team. Third baseman Shawn, the pitcher, and the catcher left during lunch to enjoy pizza at Papa Gino's ... right across the street from school and next door to Shaw's Supermarket. After lunch, they bought sunflower seeds at Shaw's and sat on the outside bench spitting shells. Not so smart they discovered as Shawn's English teacher greeted them on her way into the supermarket. They were reported and all three members had to endure the two-and-a-half hour ride to the game in Nauset to sit on the bench.

Kalin's teen troubles were always drama at its best ... or worst. She also had bouts with school skipping, a crime of high punishment in our house since both Paul and I are educators. There was the time when I returned from school and saw her nursing a very bad sunburn. She swore it was inflicted on her during the 15 minutes it took to watch her teacher's toddler peacefully sleeping in the car while the teacher ran into the school for something forgotten. This happened at 3:30, well past sunburn danger in early May. And of course there was the time she intercepted her progress report ... and for good reason. She was not doing well. Actually, her marks were just shy of miserable ... and so was she when I made her leave a swim meet early. I was too angry to speak except for one sentence, spoken in the controlled voice of a parent ready to explode; "Just how does one fail music?"

> *Being 13 wouldn't be complete without the testing of boundaries and limits, but for those of us who have been through this more than once, we're tired.*

This leads us to Michael, in the midst of 13-year-old-hell. We don't have those kinds of stories to tell ... yet. I will say it remains an awkward age though. With a top jaw too small for all of his teeth, a body that continues to grow in speed that defies logic, and the ongoing fight with his skin, he has his struggles. Being 13 wouldn't be complete without the testing of boundaries and limits, but for those of us who have been through this more than once, we're tired.

So when the orthodontist put in a metal torture device that I was responsible for turning each day to stretch his palate painfully, I will admit that I derived a teeny bit of pleasure. For the times I know I will wait up for him and for the calls from school because of a skipped class or two, I felt entitled to inflict a little bit of parental sadism.

The torturing is now done, leaving his crowded teeth a thing of the past. Replacing the overlaps are now spaces roughly the size of Rhode Island. But he has a positive outlook having perfected the art of spitting in all sorts of new ways. As for the lack of aesthetics, he's battling that by dressing up for school. Most parents would be thrilled but like I said, we're tired and this means that nightly, we have to check out what he will wear the next day ... every 45 seconds while offering praise or assistance. We also have to touch his hair in the morning to make sure the gel he has applied will cause impalement of anyone who comes too close. But if this is the worst I have to contend with for the last of my brood, I'm happy to look, smile, and skewer a finger or two for the sake of getting through the tumultuous time of my last teenager. ◉

Mother of the Year
KATHY KENNEY-MARSHALL

A few weeks ago, I wrote a column about whether or not it's ever ok to have a favorite child. After reading the column, my kids had a few thoughts, most of which I won't bore you with. However, one of my offspring, while reading about a time when he most definitely was *NOT* my favorite, muttered just loud enough for the neighbors to hear if their televisions were blaring and there was a parade of fire engines blazing by the house, "And what? Like you're Mother of the Year or something?" I was shocked not by the comment itself, but at the thought that he knew about my secret life-long dream! And worse, that he actually suggest it wasn't a possibility! But since I had put their actions out for public scrutiny, I suppose it's only fair that I expose my own successes and failures as well.

It's difficult to be objective when it comes to parenting. There are millions of pages written on the subject, yet by the very definition of human nature, it's almost impossible to define what would make the practically perfect parent. When they are younger, it's a little easier I suppose. As long as they are fed, bathed often enough to prevent disease, and kept out of moving traffic, you're doing your job. A nomination is possible as long as the judges of the contest believe that a four year old can fill out the five page form that ends with a three paragraph cohesive essay singing your praises. They didn't and I lost.

As my daughter, the oldest, reached school age, I thought I had another shot. I held her down every morning so I could comb her hair. I dressed her in outfits that mostly matched, and I carefully packed her lunchbox with a nutritious sandwich of tuna (healthy omega-3 fish oils ... 50 points!) with low-fat mayonnaise, a banana (there was still a little yellow showing some days), and a thermos filled with Crash-Bang-Boom-Round-Your-Classroom Fruit Drink that contained not less than one percent real fruit juice *AND* more importantly a vegetable (everyone knows that high-fructose corn syrup contains corn, a vegetable ... right?). What probably cost me the prize that year was the time I ran out of mayonnaise and used ketchup on her sandwich. And I ran out of tuna. So apparently peanut butter and ketchup sandwiches are not Mother of the Year lunches. Especially if you also forgot to fill the thermos with juice and put day old coffee in it instead. Everyone has an off day now and then.

So I needed to try again in other wonderful ways to prove my parenting prowess. I read about and tried reverse psychology once. I gave my children, ages 3, 8 and 10 at the time, Snickers bars for dinner. I told them they could have their spinach and eggplant casserole for dessert if they finished all their dinner. No dessert for them that night. No Mother of the Year for me either.

The next year, I went on a total health food kick. This was the ticket I was certain. No more sugar, no more juice, nothing that wasn't natural or organic. They balked and complained, but the last straw was the Lentil Loaf I made on Halloween. They had to eat it or I would not give in and let them go trick-or-treating and actually eat that horribly unhealthy candy. They ate the loaf, (or perhaps the dog ate it, I'm still not quite sure). And to make myself an even better, more educational mother, I incorporated a math lesson into the fun of Halloween; they had to make a graph to show what candies were the most popular. My four-year-old failed at this task and to this day hates both Halloween and math. Apparently this was not the way to Mother of the Year stardom either.

So I finally decided to quit trying, or rather quit being so obvious about it. For example, instead of rushing my son to the hospital after a Pop Warner football injury that made his wrist swell to the size of a small grapefruit, I relaxed. I simply gave him a bag of frozen peas to put on it and sent him to bed. He woke me at 3am with thawed peas stuck to the side of his head and his wrist now resembled a watermelon. I still did not panic. I gave him some Motrin, a bag of frozen corn and sat with him on the couch until he fell asleep (10 points for sitting on the couch with him!). By morning however, as he sat crying in pain, I decided that it was time to seek medical attention, (more points). He forgave me when the cast came off six weeks later. I was back on the list of nominees ... almost. But this was getting tiring.

Now my children are 19, 17, and 12. I try my best to do what feels right and I have come to accept, (sort of), that since they are growing up to be such great people,(even through the purple hair and nose piercing phases), maybe I don't really need an award to know that I've done a good enough job as a mom. What is really important is as simple as letting them know how much I love them. I'm not perfect, but isn't perfection overrated? I'm ok at this mothering thing and that will have to do.

And if it's not, well, there's always next year! ⊙

CRUMBS from The Classroom

Lifelong Learning: The Greatest Gift

KATHY KENNEY-MARSHALL

There are so many stories behind the walls of a classroom. Like most teachers, I find myself talking about my encounters with kids whenever I'm out of the classroom with friends, family, and even a stranger in the grocery store. Classroom life seems to connect to situations wherever I find myself talking with people. When you're in the teaching profession, you can't help it, because teaching is not just a job you do, it a lifestyle that you live. You wake up thinking about your 'kids'. You wonder through the morning rituals of lunch making and breakfast eating, how the day will unfold before you. The most experienced and well prepared teacher knows that more often than not, because of the very nature of children, your day just happens to you.

You may walk through the front door of your school and find out that you're getting a new student. If, as it is becoming more prevalent, he comes to you with no records from his previous school(s), you have no idea how long he will stay. He may have been brought to a shelter in the middle of the night because his father was abusive. He may not have any clothes but the ones on his back and he's probably scared and angry. You will have to mother him before you can teach him anything. He may come the day before you are giving state exams and though he can barely read, you have to make him take it anyway. You don't know anything but his name, so you do what all good teachers do; you punt.

First you must make him feel at home and assure him that he's in a safe welcoming place. By the time the bell rings there is a desk ready for him complete with folders, books, pencils, and a name tag with his name spelled correctly. You ask if he has a nickname and you put a label on his new locker with it. You make sure he has a "buddy", someone extra kind in the class to lead him around his new routine. You do all this like a pro and in two weeks, after wreaking havoc on his new classmates because of his desperate situation and uncontrollable anger, he is gone; lost in the sea of others like him who disappear without an ending to his story. You also missed the beginning. But for two weeks, you lay in bed each night worrying about him even though he tried to hit you with his math book. You remember him because even he, after such a short time, has made an imprint on who you are. Teachers are ever evolving, changing slightly with the best and the worst of classes. What we need to do is remain mindful of the impact we have on our kids ... and the impact they have on us.

> *The most experienced and well prepared teacher knows that more often than not, because of the very nature of children, your day just happens to you.*

What I have come to know is that people in the private sector of employment are one of two kinds: teacher lovers, or people who are scornful of our career choice. The lovers remark about the difficulty of our jobs, the heartbreak we take home with us when one of our "flock" struggles, and the enormity of the contact we have on the lives of the future. The scorners in contrast hold the strong opinion that we have it easy; that we skate through nine and a half months of the year only to luxuriate in laziness during school vacations and summer months. The lament is that their 9-5s are the 'real' jobs in society because, really, who can call a six-hour a day job full time? I've heard it all in the 18 years I have been an educator and to be truthful, I *DO* love my summers off. Being a mother, it afforded me the opportunity to be with my children more than those mothers who had year round employment. And I was able to be home in time to cook dinner at a reasonable time when they were small enough to eat at the early-bird-special hour of 5:00.

But make no mistake, teaching isn't easy and it certainly isn't a job that starts at 9:00 and ends at 3:00. It is as fulfilling as anything I could ever imagine, but it is much more difficult than anything I was taught about in college as well. What I know in my heart from my days with children is that most of what we do is on the job training. What I learned in college were the standards that I needed to abide by as a teacher. I learned how to prepare lessons with goals and objectives. I had to learn teaching philosophies and methodology. I learned the "lingo" that was popular at the time. Most folks can learn those basic lessons. But what you need most to be a teacher cannot be taught in any book. What I have found to be most valuable is the experience the children bring me every single day.

Lifelong Learning: The Greatest Gift

In looking back on those college years, my favorite professors were elementary school teachers themselves once. I loved most when they shared stories of their experiences in their early days as teachers. I learned that anyone can look at a teacher's manual and carry out the lesson, but not everyone can teach.

I've had teachers in training work in my classroom. I've had college kids whose first classroom experience was with me. I've always tried to guide them with clarity and honesty, explaining the reality of classroom life. I've had adults who have changed careers in their forties and are at the end of their degree program. They come to be student teachers and realize that it's not so easy to stand in front of a group of eight-year-olds and hold their attention. They find themselves scared to death even though they may have run successful million dollar businesses. They learn quickly that there is no manual in the world that makes you a teacher.

So what I hope to impart are some of the experiences that made me who I am as a teacher so far. I am not complete any more than those youngsters I teach. That is the foundation of the joy in being a teacher; we get to continue to emerge not only as teachers, but as people while the children teach us lessons that are as important as the ABCs. Lifelong learning … what a gift. ☉

Class Pests and Pets
KATHY KENNEY-MARSHALL

Once upon a time, in my early teaching years, I was full of wonderful yet stupid ideas. When teaching about the Hopi Tribes of the Southwest for example, we saved milk cartons and boxes to make actual pueblos. We glued the boxes together after cutting out smoke-holes, then concocted a mud-paper maché to cover them with. Thankfully, we did not have carpets in our classrooms back then but the mess seemed to spread from wall to wall. I made sure I was out of the building by the time the custodians made their rounds because I was certain that they would hand me a scrub brush and a mop to clean it up myself though I think they should have been grateful instead for the overtime pay they received due to my class pueblo project.

Another bright idea I had was to have a class pet. Some teachers had aquariums in their rooms and occasionally there was a guest hamster, gerbil, or some sort of creature. I liked the idea of a pet, but hamsters were not my cup of tea nor were fish. I wanted something we could not only take care of, but something that we could learn from as well. I chose to get a guinea pig happily supplied to us by the Science Resource Dept.

Her name was voted on by the children and Heather became a part of our classroom family. The children took turns changing the cage each week and they were all too happy to feed her every day. I would walk around the room holding her while I taught and quite often, if I noticed a particular child in need of a little bit of extra love that day, Heather was deposited on that child's lap for the duration of the lesson.

She had a sweet temperament and appeared to enjoy the endless attention from the kids. But in reading about guinea pigs, I learned that they are extremely social and flourish when other guinea pigs shared their cage. I felt guilty when I left for the weekend each Friday so I thought she deserved a companion.

Believing in creating teachable moments I thought that we should get a male guinea pig. This way, we could have baby guinea

Class Pests and Pets

pigs and I could create wonderful lessons using them. We could weigh them and graph their growth. We could observe them and write about their activities. But as I said, I was fairly new to the teaching business and there are times when I should keep my "great" ideas to myself.

When I announced to the class that a male guinea pig was going to join us, they were very excited. I explained that we would not only be supplying a friend to Heather, but the two of them would eventually have babies and we would be able to watch them grow up. I didn't count on the question that came from Amanda.

"How will they have babies, Mrs. KM? Don't they have to get married first?" This was in the early 90s when many of the children still had parents who told them that in order to have children, you had to be married. Who was I to pass moral judgment on those families who did not agree in the marriage first principle? I had to think quickly.

"Well, ah, yes Amanda. They can be married." Thus ocurred the first ever guinea pig wedding.

Sophia's parents ran a bakery in Boston and since there was to be a wedding, she begged them to make a wedding cake. Jenny made beautiful paper roses and brought them in the next week complete with white vases.

The children wanted to know what we would do at the "wedding".

"Will she wear a dress?" asked Kevin

"Ah, no Kevin," I responded. "Guinea pigs don't wear clothes."

"Will they have a honeymoon?" Ashley wanted to know.

"Honey, they're guinea pigs. They aren't allowed on planes unless they are accompanied by human beings. So no, there won't be a honeymoon."

"Can we have champagne?" asked Harry. This was getting out of hand.

I decided I would try to cater to the kids a bit and make another lesson out of it. I would provide sparkling grape juice for a toast, but for this toast, each child would have to do a little reading and find one fact about guinea pigs. I was surprised at the things they found. So far, so good.

Finally the day of the "wedding" arrived. Scales, the groom, had long black hair, while Heather was of the short haired white variety. I hoped that the parents, who thought I had lost my mind, might notice my open-minded celebration of diversity. Since it was Amanda and Jake's turn to take care of the couple for the week, they took extra care to comb the tangles out of Scales's hair and make sure Heather's coat was shiny.

Apparently though, Scales did not have the temperament for this detangling process we discovered when Jake had to run to the nurse after being bitten by the disgruntled groom. Joey, thinking that Scales probably found Heather too ugly to marry, announced his epiphany to the class and proceeded to roll on the floor laughing at his own joke. Several other boys became excited and added that he didn't want to get 'cooties' from her. The girls were offended and made their feelings known. The bride left unattended while the girls screeched at the boys, became spooked by the melee and ran.
Another lesson was learned; frightened guinea pigs are quite good at hide-and-seek. Joey had to sit out in the hall for starting it all until 20 minutes later when we were able to capture her from under a table.

When all was calm, Sophia's father came in with ... and I'm not embellishing even a little ... a real wedding cake complete with pillars and white roses that cascaded down the sides. Sophia was very proud, while I, truth be told, was a little embarrassed. I know how much work went into that cake and I just wasn't sure that a wedding for the two rodents in front of me was worth all the fuss. In looking at the children's eyes however, I realized that this was something they would not soon forget.

The principal arrived and the wedding began complete with a tape of the Wedding March. Thankfully, the kids did not expect a walk down the aisle and the table they were put on, (covered with a white tablecloth soon to be stained yellow and littered with items resembling ice cream jimmies), was acceptable. As we held our glasses and each child gave his or her fact, I was pleasantly surprised to see the look of delight on the principal's face. He was impressed at what the children were able to learn about guinea pigs. His own toast was not a fact he had found, but a compliment to the children and well wishes for the happy couple. We ate cake, drank sparkling grape juice and the children took turns patting the newlyweds. About 60 days later, I walked in the classroom to find five new members of our class.

Class Pests and Pets

When the children walked in, they were elated to see what had occurred the night before. The babies were promptly named and brought the mundane lessons on measurement and addition to life. This turned out better than I had imagined.

We did face two problems with the new family. First, male guinea pigs often try to eat their young which explains why there has never been a Father-of-the-Year nomination for a guinea pig. We had to find a new cage, or rather a free cage quickly. We settled for an old aquarium the custodian found in the basement.

The second was more problematic. Rodents of all sorts do 'their business, frequently. With two guinea pigs, the odor by Friday was quite noticeable as soon as anyone entered the room. Add five more urinating pooping creatures and the aroma was downright pungent. Cleaning the habitats became a daily ritual and was taking up far too much time, not to mention the fact that I had lessons to teach the cleaners. I found myself counting the days until I could give the babies to the children. Luckily, guinea pigs are born with hair and teeth, so I didn't have to wait long.

We had a guinea pig raffle since so many students brought in permission slips to become pet owners. That Friday, five lucky children left with their new loved ones in shoe boxes while I consoled the 19 others who left with only their homework.

There were good times certainly and bad times as well. Our school building was under construction and we had to move across the street to the former high school until it was ready for occupancy. As a high school it was fine. The halls were larger, the classrooms smaller, and the desks were certainly not elementary size or shape. But worse than that for our class pets was the fact that in our temporary shelter, there was no sink. Cleaning the cages and grooming the animals proved more difficult than ever. But we managed until one fateful day when two boys, children who were not trusted to handle anything living unless closely supervised, had an idea.

One day during recess, under the guise of having bathroom emergencies, they entered the empty classroom to give Scales a haircut. Not knowing how to handle a wriggling guinea pig *AND* a pair of scissors, they nicked him in the hair cutting process. Though there wasn't much blood, they were frightened into doing what any eight-year-old would do in that situation; they threw the scissors away, put the screeching guinea pig back in the cage, and ran.

    I didn't notice until a few days later when I became concerned at the animal's change in behavior. He was lethargic. He wouldn't eat and there was goop coming out of his eyes. I couldn't see bringing him to the vet, so instead, I brought him to the pet store from which he came. The owner took one look at him and grabbed him from me. During a thorough exam, he discovered a cut on the poor guy's genitals. The amateur barbers had literally almost neutered him. The kind pet shop owner gave me parakeet antibiotic and assured me that he would be fine in a few days.

    It wasn't hard to figure out who had done the damage and the punishment was as severe as it can get for a third grader; parents were called, the principal was summoned, and they lost recess for a week. But, on the flip side, a guinea pig homicide was averted and once recovered, Scales was as good as new, though now we had to work a bit harder catching him whenever he saw anyone holding a comb to groom his long hair

    After having several more litters, each one smaller than the one before, I decided that I had had enough of the class pet nonsense. While the children derived great pleasure from the three years of successful experiments, I was tired of the whole thing. But how would I tell the class?

    My principal saved me by approaching me one morning as soon as I entered the school. With the renovation complete, our school was equipped with an alarm system that used a sensor detector. Little did I know how in love (horny) Heather and Scales were. My boss approached the topic delicately. He explained that we had the new alarm and that it had gone off several times at night, sometimes after midnight. This brought the police on the scene and the custodian would be paged to let them into the school. It took several visits from the local constabulary and several hefty "off-hour" payments for lengthy searches of the entire building. As it turns out, it was Heather and Scales who set off the motion detector each time. So in the words of my boss, I had to get rid of the "copulating" rodents immediately.
I was off the hook.

    Since then, I have not offered to play hostess for any more class pets though from time to time, a former guinea pig lottery winner writes to invite me to the funeral of "Wiggles" or "Snickers." Sadly, I am always unavailable though I do send a card. ◉

The First Year

KATHY KENNEY-MARSHALL

I began my classroom teaching at a parochial school in the inner city. All but three of the student body were black children from various areas of the globe. Some, though not many, were African American. Most of the others were from Haiti, Cape Verde, Barbados, and the Bahamas to name a few. My two children came to school with me at St. Matthew's and it was a wonderful experience for all of us.

I started teaching kindergarten. I had 29 full-day students with no teacher aide. But it was a wonderful experience for me because these children were so well behaved. I remember my interview with the principal, Sister LMNOP, who somberly told me that these children would probably not be as bright as my own children as English was not their first language. I was surprised at her judgment and respectfully disagreed. It seemed to me that since my own children could only speak one language, these children had the advantage. The interview opened my eyes about my new boss as well; she viewed the students in her school as a substandard group of children. It made me a little sad to think that someone in the religious arena could be so narrow minded. But that was not my main concern. I was excited to start the school year and meet these children.

My first impressions were accurate the day they filed silently into my room. They were a little nervous but soon I had them smiling as we played a name game. Since it was kindergarten, I had the luxury of getting to know them slowly without the pressure of a heavy academic curriculum to conquer. Certainly there were guidelines and lessons I would be responsible for. But having the students all day as opposed to the two and a half hours that most public schools at that time had, gave me a little extra time to let them learn through play.

We got along so well and I loved each one of them. They were obedient and gracious. If I brought treats in on Friday, they needed no reminders to say thank you. When naptime came, they dutifully reclined on their mats and fell asleep to quiet music I played. When naptime was over, we had story time. It didn't take long to develop a routine that we were all comfortable with. Sister LMNOP, I found, didn't really care what we did as long as the students were quiet and the shades were exactly half way up. It was a wonderful start.

We had recess twice a day where they were allowed to make noise and we played Duck, Duck, Goose almost every day. But I soon realized that Sister LMNOP was completely serious about the quiet aspect of the classroom when one afternoon after a joyful game of tag, Stephie came skipping into the room. In a blur, Sister came bustling by me, grabbed the child by the arm, and walloped her behind. Everyone was stunned into silence. Sister then turned to me and said, "There will be no skipping in our classrooms." All I could do was nod and wait for her to leave. I began to realize that the strict atmosphere of the school would take a toll on me, if not the children.

It was Stephie who taught me another lesson that first year. It was mid-April during story time. The sleepy children, all in various stages of wakefulness stumbled over to the story area while I began to read. In the middle of *Where The Wild Things Are*, Stephie jumped up and yelled,

"Mrs. Marshall! Your face!"

Since we had lunch before naps I thought perhaps I had some mayonnaise or something on my chin. I asked her what was wrong with my face and proceeded to wipe my hand around my mouth and chin. She stood with her hand on her own face and said in shock,

"It's white!" I chuckled and replied, "Yes, Stephie, my face is white. I'm white. Did you just notice that?" She smiled and hugged me while whispering, "I like white teachers."

Her five year old eyes were still color blind as far as differences in race. I was touched and amused as I told her that I liked her too.

When I could no longer afford to work at the parochial school where I had to supplement my income as a waitress on nights and weekends, I realized I had to leave St. Matthew's. Though my children were at school with me, I knew that working two jobs was taking a toll on our family. By my second year there, my husband, Paul, was also teaching in St. Matt's middle school. He also worked two jobs. We both wanted another child but knew that we couldn't afford to have a third nor would we have the time to spend with our kids if we continued working there. I sadly gave my notice and thought about becoming a full-time waitress until I could become a public school teacher.

I didn't have long to wait. That summer, I was hired to teach in Framingham, Massachusetts in the third grade at McCarthy Elementary School. It was a dream come true. ◉

The Thing About Kellie
KATHY KENNEY-MARSHALL

Ask any teacher, any honest teacher anyway, if he or she likes all of their students and the answer will most likely surprise you. Teachers are supposed to like children, otherwise, why go into teaching?

I posed a question to one of my third grade classes one day:

Do you think teachers have favorite students? They were horrified at the question. "No!" they all shouted at once. One girl followed that with, "You're not supposed to have favorites. My mother says that you're supposed to like us all the same." She looked worried. Being one of the most enjoyable classes I'd taught, I thought I'd play with them a bit.

"Well, that's not true; I don't like you all the same because you're all different. I like you, Shelly, because you're funny and try hard. I like Jay because he listens so well. I like all of you for different reasons. But I still have a favorite." I told them.

"Who is it?" they all wanted to know. I smiled wickedly at them and replied, "Whoever irritates me the least that day!"

I knew this group would find this brand of humor funny though it isn't so with every group. Each day thereafter, they would ask me as we waited for the dismissal bell who my favorite was that day. I would actually choose someone though keeping track was a challenge. Everyone had a chance to be my favorite on various days for various reasons. On the very first day of what became known as THE QUESTION, I chose the most 'challenging' child in my class. He looked shocked as did the other 22 children waiting to hear my answer.

In looking through his records before school began and in speaking with his former teachers, I found out that Michael was always the worst kid in class. If something was stolen, it was Michael. If there was teasing, it was done by Michael. If there was a disruption, it would certainly involve Michael. He was smart; I was told, but totally uncontrollable. Hmmm, an uncontrollable eight-year-old? I was intrigued.

When school started, Michael did, in fact, test my patience daily, but the rest of the class balanced that out as they seemed genuinely eager to hear everything I had to say, (and they laughed at all of my jokes which made them instantly loveable). From time to time, I would send Michael out in the hall for his outbursts, and then, being the meanie that I am, I'd play an impromptu game of Simon Says. Michael was indeed smart as he realized that it was more fun to be in the classroom than out in the hall alone, even if we were doing class work instead of playing games. Consequently, his behavior improved.

So on that first day of THE QUESTION, I chose Michael and explained to the class that I chose him because even though I had to speak to him several times that day for calling out an answer and forgetting to raise his hand, I recognized and admired that he was trying so hard to improve his behavior. I told them all that it's not easy to change something when it becomes a habit. Even poor behavior choices become habit because it's what others expect out of you. Michael had to believe that he wasn't the worst boy in class and even better? That afternoon he was the favorite, a title that he never thought he'd earn. I asked him how it felt to be my favorite that day. He just smiled and quietly told me that it felt 'real good'. The rest of the class clapped for him and congratulated him. That's the kind of kids they were.

So each day that year they'd ask, and I would pick someone and find something that would be favorite-worthy of that child. But the next year, I did not have a class that could handle such an endeavor. It was a tough group by any standard. But I was determined that if I couldn't play the game of favorites, I would try my best to find something likable about each of my new students.

With some kids, it's easy. The likeability just jumps out of them and grabs you by the heartstrings. There were about seven out of that class of 21 that were not so obvious. I had to work hard to find it. In Ted, who came to school disheveled, dirty, and had trouble following any direction, I found generosity. The boy came to school four days out of five without a snack, but on the day he had one, he was the first to share with someone who forgot theirs. In Annie, who had the bad attitude of a 14 year old, I found a poet. When I sat alone with her and calmly talked about the tantrum she just threw, along with a bucketful of plastic coins, I realized that she had a reasonable side that was indeed wise beyond her eight years. When we wrote in class, her words showed me the little girl inside.

The Thing About Kellie

Slowly but surely, I found something about each that I genuinely liked ... except for Kellie. With Kellie, it was much harder and the harder I tried to find the quality in her worthy of admiration, the more it eluded me. She was sullen and moody. She complained about everyone and everything. The other kids looked at her papers, she would whine. Nobody liked her she would complain. It seemed that the person who didn't like Kellie most was Kellie. But Kellie didn't have that ability to have an open discussion like Annie. The world hated her and nothing was ever fair in her opinion which she treated as fact.

Every morning as I greeted the class at the door and handed out their morning math paper, I smiled at Kellie and tried to compliment her. It wasn't difficult to find something nice to say about her appearance, she was always beautiful. She was tall, had lovely brown hair, and always wore clean clothes that matched just so. But even these compliments were met with negativity. If I told her that her hair looked nice, she would reply that she hated the barrettes. If I said that her shirt was adorable, she answered that her mother made her wear it. By the end of October, I began to think perhaps there are kids in the world that I just couldn't like but would have to learn to live with. But then conference time arrived.

I had an appointment with Kellie's mom at 3:00 one Thursday afternoon. At 3:10, I thought perhaps she had forgotten and I started down to the teachers' room to get a drink. Halfway there, a parent nearly knocked me over in her rush to get to a classroom. It was Kellie's mom.

All the way back to the classroom, she talked a mile a minute. "I'm sorry I'm late, the traffic was a bitch and my boss wouldn't let me out early. I work ova at the Leatha Store, ya know. Oh God, do you have a body for leatha ... a paira leatha pants would looks pissa on you. Jesus, Kellie wishes I'd wear stuff like the outfit you got on. Look at me ... she'd be so embarrassed."

She had on a tie-dyed T-shirt with the Rolling Stones signature lolling tongue hanging out all over her chest. Yes, I thought, Kellie might be embarrassed because I knew my kids would be. But working parents don't always have time to be fashion plates outside of work, this much I knew.

When we reached the classroom, she heaved her suitcase size bag onto the table as she plopped herself down in a chair. Her cell phone went off and she yelled at someone on the other end before finally giving me her attention. I will never forget the first words she said as she sat there; "So ... about Kellie, huh? I know, I know, my kid's an asshole." There it was. I sat back and smiled having finally found the thing I liked about Kellie ... she had a mother who thought she was an asshole and wasn't afraid to say so to a perfect stranger. Her own mother had in four strong words told me all I need to know in order to change how I dealt with her.

When I found my voice my mouth smiled, but in my eyes were daggers as I said, "No, Mrs. J, I don't think she is at all. As a matter of fact, your daughter is beautiful, smart, and has amazing social skills. You should be very proud of her."

Now it was Mrs. J's turn to be shocked into silence. Sadly, it lasted only a moment. She agreed with the beautiful part, but of course there was a down side to that too; she'd be hell as a teen.

And on it went for 30 minutes, me showing Kellie's strengths, her mother making excuses why she wasn't really that good. As I spoke so positively about Kellie, I found a genuine affection growing for this little girl who had to live with this every single day and yet, she still came to school and did her work, albeit with an Eeyore-like attitude. But who could blame her? The concept of a self-fulfilling prophesy was rearing its ugly truth in front of my eyes.

It took a bit longer for Kellie to start to believe me when I said nice things to her, but eventually she did. And eventually, she began to smile a little, then a little more. She never did completely lose that sense of gloom and the notion that nobody liked her; it was a crutch she had leaned on for too long ... compliments of her mom. But another side of Kellie, the side that had hidden for so long dared to peek out from time to time.

Now, several years later, Kellie comes to visit me after school once in a while. She still complains a bit and is a tad whiney, but the thing about Kellie and her ability to maneuver through a less than fair world, is more than likeable, it's something that I am so proud of her for. ◉

Captain Underpants: More Than Just a Funny Book

KATHY KENNEY-MARSHALL

Certain words in the English language are difficult to use in every day conversation, yet fit certain situations perfectly. The word *flummoxed* is such a word. I love the sound of it, yet in the teachers' room or at my own dining room table, it is not often that I get to use it so appropriately as when I tell this story; a story that literally left me flummoxed. Its synonyms, *baffled, stunned, bewildered,* even *flabbergasted* never felt quite right. After reading this story, see if you agree and if you would also become flummoxed if put in the same situation. I swear every word is true.

Every year is like a new chapter in a book of short stories. The characters change and with that change, a teacher must find ways to teach those in her charge in ways befitting the chemistry and dynamics of the group. One year, I found my skills as an educator painfully stretched.

My class of 23 students had nine children who made my life that year more stressful than I thought possible. They were loud, impolite, and difficult to control. Even though I had always believed that my strength in teaching was my ability to maintain control and therefore deliver my lessons in meaningful ways, this group of nine made me think that perhaps I was giving myself too much credit. I realized early in the year I would need more than a positive behavior chart to reign in this crew. I was also fearful that their misbehaviors would lessen the experience for the 14 other children. I tried everything I could think of, yet even when I had acceptable mornings, it was my class that the cafeteria aides had the most trouble with every single day. Perhaps they could only pull themselves together for the first half of the day. Or maybe, I needed to incorporate more physical activity into my lessons. Whatever it was, I had to try something different.

Before the "No Child Left Behind" drivel, and before the directives from non-teachers in the government who mandated "time on task" decrees, children were given two 15 minute breaks called recess. The first recess occurred during the midmorning time when kids were allowed to eat a snack and get some fresh air. The second came after lunch so once again, they could get some fresh air and run off some of the calorie laden lunches modern schools serve. Though super nachos and pancake on a stick were favorites, the fat content alone could put a student into a calorie induced coma if it were not for recess time.

> *Once again, my class was "the worst class in the history of school." They exaggerated, but not by much.*

Recess was also a time for teachers who did not have patrol duty to have a few minutes of prep time. In elementary schools, it is common for educators to have 30 minutes or fewer of preparation time each day. We teach every subject area, yet are expected to prepare perfect lessons within these 20-30 minute slots. We are, after all, super human beings. So as important as recess is for children it is also vital for teachers. It took huge indiscretions on the part of a child for a teacher to take either of those breaks away from her students.

As you can imagine, I was at the point of desperation when, once more I was met by two disgruntled cafeteria aides one afternoon. Once again, my class was "the worst class in the history of school." They exaggerated, but not by much. I decided that drastic measures must be taken when I informed the group that they would be eating lunch with me in the classroom for a lesson in lunchroom decorum.

My classroom was set up in a horseshoe shape with one row of the frequent offenders' desks set in a row within the middle of the shoe. They would eat with me, be taught manners, (thank you, Mom) and because of my loss of valuable prep time, they would also lose their recess. I couldn't sleep the night before so dreaded was the lunch period to follow the next day.

All went well ... sort of. I put on my firmest angry third grade teacher face and sat in front of them. They had napkins on their laps and all were instructed to chew with mouths closed. They were to use utensils, a novelty to some even though it was pasta day, and there was to be no talking whatsoever.

It was about 15 minutes into this silent lunch when Ace, sitting in the frequent offender row, raised his hand tentatively asking to go to the nurse.

Captain Underpants: More Than Just a Funny Book

With my unsympathetic face plastered on, I asked if he was sick. This was the interchange:
    Ace: "I need the nurse."
    Me: "Are you sick?"
    Ace: "No." His eyes were nervously looking back and forth.
    Me: "Then what's wrong with you?" (with as much compassion as an irritated educator could muster.)
    Ace: (whispering) "I'm stuck."
    The angry teacher look disappeared and was replaced by the emergence of confusion. I walked over to him and whispered back,
    Me: "What do you mean ... stuck?"
    Ace: "My pants."
Anger dissolved and panic began to spread through every fiber of my body. This was years before the movie, *Something About Mary,* and though I was naïve, I had a bad feeling about this. A very bad feeling.
    I ran to the hall instructing Ace, "Don't move!" As if! As luck would have it, a fellow teacher happened down the hall and I begged her to take my class to the library ... or anywhere as I had a zipper emergency. I barked orders to the rest of the class that lunch was over and they were to line up quickly.
    In the litigious society we live in, I was fearful to get too close to Ace. I called for back-up. I thought, in my female way of thinking, that a male would be better suited to this situation than I. Dick, the guidance counselor, came to the rescue; until he heard what was wrong.
    "Medical!" was his only word as I described my situation. The nurse was called. I remained at a safe distance, the doorway, until my help arrived. She asked me to join her while she tried to free his "maleness" from the offending zipper. Their conversation was beyond my "need-to-know" lexicon of student-teacher information.
    Nurse: Ace, you aren't wearing underwear. Why?"
    Ace: "I couldn't find any."

Nurse: "Oh! I see you aren't circumcised."

I remember thinking, "I don't know this, I don't know this! LALALALALA."

The next request was that I make "the call." I asked if our classroom phones could reach 911. The nurse responded as if I were a five year old.

"Call his parents!"

Sadly for me, and his parents, was the fact that they spoke little English. Somehow, his father seemed to understand the words, *stuck*, and *pants*. Ace had to be brought out of the school in a wheelchair.

By the end of the day, the entire faculty and staff had learned of this discomfiting experience. Being fairly new to the building, to say I was embarrassed is an understatement.

Ace came to school the next day to my surprise. He nodded at me as he entered the building showing me that his attire was much more appropriate that day. He had on sweatpants. With or without underwear remains a mystery, but I prefer it that way.

On the final day of school, the teachers had a luncheon where gifts were given to departing teachers and jokes about the year were laughed about. That year, I received a high honor among teachers; a joke gift that left me speechless. A colleague cut the front panel off of a pair of jeans. Through the zipped up zipper was an elongated oval of pantyhose stuffed with cotton.

This was the perfect ending to a perfectly awful year. Thank God for humor, but for the offending teacher who has not yet retired a loving caveat: Payback's a bitch! ☉

A Noble Endeavor

KATHY KENNEY-MARSHALL

A child psychologist, who presented at a seminar I recently attended, said that "Kids do well if they *CAN* and if they can't, there is something getting in the way." He cited examples of expectations that were simply out of a child's range of skills, but because of the child's reaction to those expectations, he was labeled difficult or willful. He cited examples all day long about what the skill deficits might entail and surprisingly, none of the skills he talked about were the first ones that came to my mind, and I dare say, to the minds of most teachers. He asserted that we, as adults, often mix up a child's will with skill. In other words, when a child chronically behaves in a way that is unacceptable, we assume he or she is being willful and disobedient when there might just be a simple explanation for the behavior. He gave the example of a boy who would, daily, run from the bus to the cafeteria knocking down whoever or whatever got in his way. The extrinsic punishments never worked; calls home, loss of recess, loss of privileges, etc. Finally, someone thought to ask him why. Why are you running off the bus every morning when clearly you get in trouble for it? Clearly, the boy knew the rule and could recite it back verbatim. And yet using the typical deterrents weren't changing the behavior. So back to the question; why was he repeating the behavior? When asked, he said quite simply, "My bus is one of the last buses to come in the morning and if I don't get to breakfast in time, they run out of _____ fill in the blank with whatever food item was his favorite." This was an 'aha!' moment for me. When we are faced with a large group of children, we don't often have the luxury of asking the questions that will help kids acquire the skills they need in order to do well, whether in academics, or more importantly, in behavior. The simple solution here was to make sure that the menu item was made available and the behavior ceased to exist. This doctor who presented suggested that we look at behavioral issues as we would look at kids with learning disabilities. If we did that, we would be forced to try to figure out what's lagging for kids who don't yet have the skills to figure out how to behave in ways we need them to.

I think quite fondly of a student I had two years ago. Ben came to me as a six year old even though I teach third grade where the students are eight or nine years old. He came only for math because he had tested out of both the first and second grade curricula in math and could probably have tested out of third grade math if he had been familiar with all of the language involved. I was teaching a homogenous grouping of strong math students and since math was his strength, I was asked if I would allow him into my class for that period each day. Allow? Here's where I tend to think differently about kids; if a child *NEEDS* an accommodation, I don't feel I have the option to say no. Whether 6 or 12 years old, if I had what he needed, he was coming.

> *Kids with Asperger's see the world in black and white, there is no gray for them and in a world full of gray, and it can be a very difficult place to navigate through with success.*

At first it was a bit anxiety provoking … for me, because what I haven't mentioned yet is that Ben has Asperger's syndrome which is on the Autism Spectrum. Without giving you a lecture about what it entails, let's just say that Ben could be a little trying if things weren't to his liking. Kids with Asperger's see the world in black and white, there is no gray for them and in a world full of gray, and it can be a very difficult place to navigate through with success. If Ben didn't see the point in doing something because it didn't interest him, a tantrum could very well ensue. With 25 of my own third graders, I was a little nervous about having such a young child in my room who might at any given moment decide he was done and cause some unwanted chaos. How was I going to do this? I decided that being proactive was the way to go. Six-year-olds don't always raise their hands and don't often remember to stay in a chair for longer than a few minutes. So I made Ben my "checker" since it was obvious from the moment he walked through the door that he was a math genius. He sat in the front of the room next to the board while others came to solve problems. I asked Ben if the student was correct and he was allowed to tell the classmate what a good job he did. After a few days, I was smitten with the Ben bug. He was bright, he smiled a lot because he loved the challenge of third grade math, and unlike lots of kids on the spectrum, and he loved to give me a hug on his way out of the room.

A Noble Endeavor

Unfortunately, the more time he spent in my room, the worse his behaviors became back in his first grade classroom. He reverted to some of the negative behaviors that caused his outbursts earlier in the year that were being more or less managed by an expert who came in to help. By December, it was decided that he would become a full time third grader because behavior wasn't an issue in my room. Going back to the theory that kids will do well if they CAN, I realized that there were conditions under which I would be lost with Ben when things got a little tough. He hated to write; ANYTHING. He complained that his hand hurt, and though he could be a little manipulative about that complaint, there was also certain validity to it; a six-year-old isn't developmentally able to keep up with the writing rigors of an eight or nine-year-old. I could work with this by having someone write for him, or I could let him use the computer. In math, when an explanation was in order, he often wrote, "IJK", which meant, "I just know." I couldn't argue that point because with an IQ in the 99th percentile, he did just know and had no idea how he knew. He also knew the entire contents of the periodic table of elements including the number of protons, neutrons, electrons, and something called quarks. He didn't know how he knew. He read his mother's nursing and science books, but at six, you don't have the understanding that some people have a photographic memory or that you are learning as you read.

Ben also lacked the skill of diplomacy, aka, how to be nice to your classmates. I have a behavior system in my classroom based on positive peer pressure. The kids can help each other out if I'm waiting for quiet and they are rewarded as a group if they do so with points on a weekly chart. Ben was in a group of children with a very nice, but incredibly talkative boy, Jon. One day as they sat, Jon noticed Ben staring at the behavior chart so he asked, "What are you staring at?" Without hesitation, Ben's response was, "I was looking at the behavior chart and thinking that if you learned to shut your big fat mouth, we'd be winning." Yes, a very rude answer on Ben's part and quite hurtful to Jon. Once again, I had to remember to ask myself, "What is getting in the way of Ben's learning that this is rude? What skill is he lacking?" If you understand that Aspy kids lack social awareness, the answer is easy; he is speaking a statement of fact, albeit inappropriately, but he had not yet learned the skill of sparing a classmate's feelings when he actually liked Jon. I used this as a teaching moment for both boys. As I talked to the wounded classmate who was crying, I explained why Ben would say such a hurtful thing. I reminded Jon that Ben needed to learn this skill because it wouldn't come naturally to him as it would to Jon because Jon learned this through experiences he had while growing up without Asperger's. Then I brought Ben out in the hall to help him start to learn the skill of diplomacy … or at least the Golden Rule! I asked Ben if he had said something hurtful to Jon. Ben looked confused and answered,

"No, Mrs. KKM. I don't think so."

Again, being a literal minded boy, Ben had no idea that his words could hurt another. So I asked the question differently, "What did you say to Jon just a few minutes ago?"

And without hesitation Ben repeated exactly what he had said not omitting the 'big fat mouth' part that many would try to avoid because they know it's not nice. I said, "Ben, look at Jon. He is crying and upset because of what you said. What you said was mean and hurtful. Look how you made your friend feel."

Two things happened, first; Ben kept full eye contact on me, an unusual action for Aspy kids, and then, upon seeing Jon's tears, reached out and touched his arm in a display of comfort. I said to Ben, "You are not a mean boy, but what you said to Jon was mean and hurtful. I am very disappointed. You need to take care of business with your friend."

I was quite surprised in hindsight that Ben understood what I meant by taking care of business, but the words, "I'm sorry," immediately followed my firm request. Jon, not understanding that apologies need not be accepted immediately if you don't want, said, "That's ok, Ben."

I jumped in right away for another important lesson because what Ben did was NOT ok and I didn't want any confusion about that fact. "No, Jon, it's not ok. It's never ok to hurt someone's feelings with mean words. You can accept his apology, but Ben, it is NOT ok to say what you said."

The bottom line here was that Ben didn't have the skill set to know what he did was wrong. Jon had every reason to feel hurt and was owed a sincere apology, which he got. So hopefully, it was a lesson for both boys and one for me.

A Noble Endeavor

If a child CAN do well they will. I do hope that I continue learning and remembering that as I continue to ask myself, 'what is getting in the way when they can't?' As for Ben? He's doing great and is learning all sorts of social skills that are making him a much more likeable classmate, although I admit, I'll always have an enormous soft spot for him. And Jon? He's still a chatterbox from what I hear from his other teachers although he's one of my favorite chatterboxes in that he has so much to offer and so much insight that still makes me very fond of him. Our lives as teachers are so interesting and full of challenges. All I can hope for are more opportunities to figure out what's getting in the way because if I can do that? I just might be able to help my kids do well ... because I'm certain they will. ☉

Headlights and Homework
KATHY KENNEY-MARSHALL

As a new school year rushes toward us, I find summer slamming to an abrupt halt. Gone will be the days of early morning walks with the dog followed by a leisurely cup of coffee on the front porch. Sure, I'll still have early morning walks; at 5:00 am though, not the more humane hour of 7. I'll also have my coffee; while on the dreaded Route 128. But as the kids buy their new pencils and crayons, school clothes to replace the ones they outgrew in the summer sun, and perhaps a new pair of sneakers, teachers too are getting ready for the year at Target or Walmart. I, for example, took full advantage of the $0.17 notebook sale this weekend. I bought their last 25 and was forced to spend, (gasp) $0.50 on an additional 25.

We have been watching back-to-school commercials for weeks now. We've been teased by the trailers of the fall season of television shows we've been awaiting. But for me, probably the most telling sign of a new school year are the nightmares of school days gone wrong. I don't know of any teacher who hasn't had them; you're late, very late, so late that you never make it to school at all and what's worse is that you never got to call your boss. You arrive at school and can't find your classroom and worse, your supplies haven't been ordered so you are unprepared and the kids behave as kids do when they are bored; unruly and rude causing you to yell at small children only to have them either ignore you or throw small items at you. Remember, this is a dream and in dreams/nightmares, children and adults are apt to do things they wouldn't ordinarily do. I did have a book thrown at me once by a student, that's true. The book was *The Lord of the Rings,* a thick one at that! It was the paperback version and he didn't have good aim so I was fine. Also I'm not a yeller by nature; it's physically impossible for me to raise my voice above a certain decibel perhaps because I was born with quiet vocal cords. Even so, these dreams wake me in a cold sweat.

But one dream/nightmare came to me for the first time a few nights ago. It started as a real memory of my first year teaching in a public school. A young boy came into class wearing a hooded sweatshirt with the hood up. I asked him to please take off the hood because hoods and hats were not allowed inside. His response had me torn between revulsion and laughter; "I can't Mrs. KM. My dad said I have to leave my hood up so the bugs won't get on the other kids." Off he went to the nurse where the father was called to collect the lice and their host. In my recent night terror, I had the "head lights" as a first grader once called the bugs in my presence. I was covered with them and no manner of shampooing or cleaning could rid me of the creatures. I woke from that dream itchy and exhausted.

> *But for me, probably the most telling sign of a new school year are the nightmares of school days gone wrong. I don't know of any teacher who hasn't had them;*

So on these, the last few nights before school begins, remember that kids are not the only ones with first day worries; we teachers, no matter how seasoned we are, also hope that the year progresses smoothly and successfully. Either that or we just don't want to get up that early for the next ten months! ⊙

Dear Matchbooks

KATHY KENNEY-MARSHALL

Anna Quindlen wrote that "every part of raising a child is humbling." This morning as I read the essay "On Being Parent" for the thousandth time, my tears were those of a teacher's that fell as I thought about the end of another school year. But before you roll your eyes, just read on and remember, I'm a mom first, the teaching is a natural second.

Another wisdom Anna imparts is "The biggest mistake I made is that I didn not live in the moment enough." While that's true of most parents as they try to navigate through croupy nights with one child while juggling the others the next day surviving on coffee and toast crusts the children leave on their plates, it also applies to teachers. We expend too much energy on a struggling child and then to make up for it, borrow against tomorrow's resources to make sure the others are cared for. Some may argue that it's not part of our job to "live in the moment," that our job is to follow curriculum and make sure the children learn. I won't argue the second part which makes our jobs so emotionally draining and sometimes beats us down. I know. I was beginning to feel that burnt out feeling several years ago. I wondered if I could possibly do this for the rest of my life. Then I met what I will now call, my matchbook class. It is to them, my student teacher, and all the children who have come after and have benefited from how they indelibly changed me, that I write this.

While it's true that the end of a school year can be hectic, there are years when, after the last pencil is packed away, it is I who wants to do cartwheels down the empty corridors, happy to be free for the summer. Then the matchbooks came. You know who you are; the ones who reignited the fire inside of me for teaching. As your fifth grade celebration propelled you toward middle school recently, I stood in the corridor with a parent, misty eyed over not seeing your faces as I walk through the crowded halls next year.

Your "McCarthy Yearbook" chronicled your time in elementary school. I also shed a few tears while writing a good by note for its pages. But somehow, it got lost in cyberspace and wasn't there. Darn. You, of all classes deserved a final note from me. So here is what I would have written if I had another chance…an abridged version…with a few words added after reading your notes to me.

> *Some may argue that it's not part of our job to "live in the moment," that our job is to follow curriculum and make sure the children learn.*

Dear Matchbooks,

First, I'd like to congratulate you. You made it! For me, the time has flown since I met you. I read your letters and I will cherish every single one of them. I sat in the kitchen that Friday morning and "saw" each of you as I read. Collin, I saw your multicolored hair as you delivered your note. I also saw your wonderful third grade freckles with the white out that I was responsible for when you finally let me try to connect them like a dot-to-dot picture. Your mother not only forgave me, but had the sense of humor to laugh. Anthony, I see your mischievous eyes and wicked smile that I've always loved. But I also see the hurt in those eyes when you were traded as a best friend for a red Starburst. I must admit, it was hard not to laugh, but I managed until I got home and told my sons. Daniel, you also had eyes that yelled shenanigans and an impressive sense of humor. I see your red face as I caught you trying to glue Anthony to his chair … with a purple glue stick! Noodle! It made my heart sing when you signed your note with my nickname for you. I see you in that adorable Christmas dress of red velvet. Sunny D. I see you shyly smiling as you walked up to my table to correct Daily Language. Katie Nana, what would I have done without you? Kevin, do I remember you? How can I ever forget? You were the catalyst for the never to be forgotten rhyme meant to scold your teacher for an annoying hair twirling habit. I am now a closet twirler … at least I try. Lauren, don't worry. Remember when I told you that I was just like you? No, you didn't annoy me; I worried about you, but knew you would be fine. Look at you now. Didi, Steph-ANIE, Bryce, Julia, Leah, Dyl, Holly, Elizabeth, and all the rest of you, remember this; you were the ones who reignited my passion for teaching, who helped me like Sunday nights and who made me want to celebrate Monday mornings with the chant; "Happy Monday!" required before you were allowed into the room. You were the first class I cried about on that last day when I looked down the empty corridor. You

Dear Matchbooks

helped make me a better teacher so that the children who came after you benefited from what you taught me about joy. I will be forever thankful to you and you will always be MY kids.

    Love,

    Mrs. KKM

    Every teacher has a similar tale, at least I hope so. Because if we are truly honest, there are years that we might feel as if the fire in our bellies for teaching feels lukewarm. But if we want it back, a single match can rekindle us … and if we're really lucky, we get a whole matchbook to insure a dazzling flame. ☉

Healthy Halloween

KATHY KENNEY-MARSHALL

It must have been a slow news week when the problem of tag on the playground made not only the pages of every paper, but it also became a story for the network morning news shows. Apparently being a kid has become a national danger. I think about recesses past when the game of Red Rover was the playground favorite. Of course many new parents aren't familiar with this game as it has become an arrestable offense in some areas of our country. In this game, teams of boys and girls held hands, formed a line, and chanted, "Red Rover, Red Rover, send Jackie right over", whereupon Jackie would run full tilt into the joined hands of the weakest link in the line in the hopes of breaking through. This is arguably why carpal tunnel syndrome and other wrist maladies have become prevalent in modern society. I can't subscribe to the notion that typing is the sole cause of wrist conditions. I have had 16 wrist surgeries to date and while I do type regularly, I played Red Rover for hours on end as a child. Red Rover was doomed as our litigious society began searching for more ridiculous ways to stifle the play time of American children.

This brings me to the holiday of Halloween. Once again, as a teacher, I prepare myself for the onslaught of sugar-laden students trampling each other through the door the morning after and sitting in an insulin-deprived hang-over by day's end. There is little learning done on the day of and the day after Halloween, so I'm quite surprised that this holiday has not yet been targeted by some radical health organization; or at least by some radical government group.

I'm especially surprised because of the recent surge in press coverage about the dangers of childhood obesity. Once again, schools were targeted as a major contributor of this trend. The government made grant monies available to schools who would use the funds to promote after school activities, (ever vigilantly safe, of course), giving children the option to move rather than sit, sloth-like but safe in front of their video games chowing down on fat-filled snacks. The same government that provides the fat-loaded, sodium-laden lunch menu items our kids are offered each day. Hmmm. I'm all for activity being a gym fanatic myself, but once again, I think common sense has been lost in this latest concern over our children's welfare.

Since schools are now "at fault" for the growing obesity in kids, many have zealously advocated that vending machines that carry soda and candy be banned from high schools. I hate to tell you, but kids are astute. If they can't get the goods at school, they'll stop and the corner store and buy them there.

Now, it is candy that is being discouraged or banned from some schools. Being a fan of candy, and a teacher who occasionally gives a Jolly Rancher or M&Ms as a reward, I find that particularly offensive. Why put the blame in one place? There's plenty of blame to go around.

Some parents use an electronic babysitter, aka TV, when they are too tired after work to take their kids to the park. Fast food places offer portion sizes that grow faster than the National Debt. Super-sizing already enormous portions of greasy fattening foods is unnecessary. By food I mean solid edible matter full of preservatives that eventually turn fat cells into obese swollen balloon-like cells bulging under our skin in the form of dimples. Yeah! Give me two orders and a roll of tape so I can skip a step and just stick them to my thighs.

Maybe we can all take a look at our roles in this important issue and look for ways of improving the future fat cells of America. Everyone needs a certain number of fat cells. We just don't need immensely engorged ones. And when kids are growing, let their bodies grow the amount they need to stay healthy, rather than feed them enough for a small village.

Though I'm just one voice in this whole argument I try to make a difference where I can by using a little common sense. With the input of my students, I offer both candy and organic vegetables when a reward is earned. They're happy and I'm thrilled that they share my love for the crunchy healthy stuff as well as an occasional mini jolt of sugar.

This brings me back to Halloween. I have a suggestion for all who wonder what to do about the pounds of candy the little goblins bring home this year; either let your kids enjoy this once a year fun holiday ritual like we all did, or start giving out organic fruits and veggies to the trick-or-treaters. You may have to scrub the dried egg and shaving cream from your house or car, but you'll have done your part in the fight against obesity in kids. I, for one, will be handing out chocolate and nothing but chocolate ... my cleaning lady doesn't do egg ☉.

Is the Sky the Limit for Everyone?
KATHY KENNEY-MARSHALL

I have a confession to make. I am a closet Howie Carr fan. There, I've just outed myself. As a Rt. 128 commuter, I am tied up in gridlock more often than I'd like, so I get a fair dose of talk radio every day. But I don't always agree and there are times I turn him off, opting for anything, even rap music over his views on public education.

Being a public educator is my chosen profession. I will not spend time "whining" about the pay, the workload, or anything else that Howie claims we complain about when "we only have to work six hours a day and for only 180 days a year for exorbitant amounts of money." I get it, people who don't teach don't know what the job entails. I love what I do despite some of the public perceptions that are erroneous at best and downright mean-spirited at its worst.

I bring this up not because of radio talk shows; it's their job to bring up controversial opinions and agitate folks. But when I read editorial letters that slam teachers and public education, I get a little mean spirited myself.

A man wrote in to this very paper claiming:

"Until someone takes on the education special interests – well paid, unionized teachers and highly paid administrators – we'll keep getting only a fraction of the educational results we pay for. Merit pay is not the least controversial in the private sector. What makes teachers – and administrators – exempt from competition?"

I'd like to answer Mr. Schofield from Ashland. Sir, I like a little healthy competition as much as you do. I sit on the edge of my seat during Red Sox–Yankee games. I love the nail-biting competition of Patriots playoff games. Competition, whether on the major league fields or the sandlot in the city is good for us. But here's the thing; when you are a teacher in a public school, you are not on an even playing field with your competitors. What's the measuring stick you want to use when giving pay based on merit?

Every year when I study my class list and meet the children who I will be responsible for that year, it doesn't take me long to figure out how much work I have in front of me. I like the challenge. It's one of my favorite parts of the job. How can I make spelling a priority for this boy from a family where he is the oldest of six and there is no father at home ? How can I find a way to help that little girl in the second row learn math when she doesn't always get to eat breakfast and lunch is still two hours away? I can be competent in content areas and still not be able to make that child less hungry. Unless of course, I take on feeding her as well as teaching her, but I'm not sure I get paid enough to feed my class every day.

Tell me how cities like Fall River, huge, poor, and full of social issues that get in the way of children's learning, can compete with the Dovers and the Wellesleys of our state? I wish all kids had the advantages of Dover and Wellesley, but to say that poor towns have the same opportunities as rich towns is just not true. It's not PC to say so, but it's honest nonetheless.

So, Mr. Schofield, if you want to support ideas like merit pay, you have to work out the kinks. You have to make the competition a little more even. Are you willing to put your money where your mouth is and find a way to help out? Life in general has the richness of difference in its people and the climates of the communities that live in them. Good public school teachers take the children who have been put in their charge and they make the most of what potentials they have. Potential ... you can't say that everybody has the same amount any more than you can say everybody has the same amount of money, intelligence, property, shoes, hair, and on and on and on. I'm very good at what I do in the classroom. I'd even boldly claim to be excellent. But you know what? I could never be a doctor, not even a lousy one. I don't have the proclivity toward the sciences and I feel faint when I see blood. My potential has its limits. So while as a teacher I can help a child reach his potential, don't kid yourself into thinking that even an exceptional teacher can make that child's potential or the situation he lives in different. The sky is not the limit for everyone in society. If it were, what a wonderful world we would be living in. Realistically, we have six hours a day to work with each child and demand excellence. The rest is up to his home and the society he lives in. Tell me, how will merit pay address that? When you have an equitable solution, give me a call. I'll be the first to sign up for merit pay, because *I DO* have the potential to offer great opportunities to kids. ◉

Gift of Poetry in Children

KATHY KENNEY-MARSHALL

There were no berets and one of the bongo players couldn't come after learning that his uncle died, but there was a plethora of poetry at McCarthy Elementary School Wednesday night. I must be crazy; I remember thinking as I typed up the program that named the 83 poets from first grade through fifth. But then again, I also found myself smiling as I typed certain names and the name of their poem. This is what teaching should be more about. Learning to love words; preparing yourself to communicate with the world through the gift of colorful language rich with thought and emotion and texture. Combine it all with a little music, a fancy outfit, and a bit of self-confidence, and you've got a night to remember.

Naomi Shihab Nie tells us in her poem, Valentine for Ernest Mann, that "poems hide ... what we must do is live in a way that helps us find them." And find them they did. From Salamanders to Skies of Blue, from the "winds of syllables that kept pulling me back" to "wondering why a plane takes off in flight". No subject is taboo to poetry. In McCarthy's cafetorium, "Hippos sprinted into heaps of sheep colored snow" and "the dandelions were readied for spring". These kids are living the lives of poets, at least for now. Taking risks to make new meanings with words that, in everyday life have different connotations. One brave poet, age 10, ventured a risk to promote the selling of her toes, while another pair of tiny first graders, wrote about Things That Are Small ... though their voices weren't and those voices that belied their owners carried all the way to the back of the standing room only crowd of parents and friends. The irony was fantastic.

I worked behind the curtain that night, popping out to hand a microphone, or turn a page in the notebook that held all of that poet's musings. I reminded them in whispers that they must speak clearly, hold the microphone just so, and more importantly, I gave them a pat on the back when they whispered, "I'm nervous Mrs. KM". I pointed to the flautists and the bongo player, who sat handsome in his suit and tie, following along intently in his own book that we wrote notes in to tell him when to play beats. I bent over the small music stand, listening from behind the curtain, ready to rescue an uncertain poet who forgot a word. There were none.

And while I listened from behind my hiding place, my own poet's heart swelled with pride for the children who courageously stood on stage in front of at least 200, with the personal words they dared write on paper and share with the world. It makes the work of this special night worthwhile when they look back at me, and smile that unforgettable I-really-did-it smile.

> *And when it was all over, after the applause, after the hugs, after the good-nights, those kids went home with a memory that poems are made of.*

And when it was all over, after the applause, after the hugs, after the good-nights, those kids went home with a memory that poems are made of. They are living life in a way that helps them find poetry. An undeniable gift wrapped in bows made with the playful nature of language and the joy of discovering how to use it. This poetry thing really is a gift. The kids who performed that night might not know it yet, but they will. As they launched into a world of wonderous words, you could see it in their young eyes ... they're hooked. While some of them may never put pencil to paper in poetic endeavors again, many will remember the night and start to keep a notebook where they jot down what they have begun to find as possible poems as they travel through their growing up journey.

Their gift of words may take them many places. Whether it takes them to Japan, the baseball diamond, or just to their bedroom to write poetry "on a flowered pink pillow", their words will fill them with a sense of wonder and fulfillment. And when they see me in the hallways at school and call out, "Mrs. KM, I wrote a poem today!" I share that joy with them knowing that power of the words of poetry. I love that they write and love that they want to share. I hope it never ends. By the way, if any of you kids are reading this ... my birthday is coming up ... I can't imagine a better gift. ☉

Parent – Teacher Time

KATHY KENNEY-MARSHALL

It's a busy time of year. The holidays are upon us carrying with them all kinds of extra activity and responsibility. It should be a happy time of family gatherings and parties with friends. But what many people, or rather people who don't have school age children don't know is that it's also parent-teacher conference time. As a parent AND a teacher, I have the drudgery ... ah, I mean the pleasure of sitting on both sides of the table.

In my school system, we handle parent conferences by scheduling several early release days into the calendar. But because most parents work, some of us come in earlier than 7 (school starts at 8:15) and stay as late as 5:00 or 6:00. Yesterday, for example, my first conference was scheduled for 7:30am at the request of the parent. Living 30 miles away from school and traveling on Rt. 128 meant that I had to leave my house by 6:15am. I made it on time ... for an invisible parent. It was the easiest conference I had all day. I understand how traffic can be, but without the benefit of a phone call, I spent my morning engaging in impolite conversation with him in my head. Having rushed to get there on time I didn't stop for coffee worrying that I might not be prepared. This alone made me just a teeny bit cranky. So I substituted the coffee with a few handfuls of chocolate (that's caffeine, right?) and ate my good mood right back into place. Stuff happens and teachers (who have caffeine) are flexible by nature (if they have caffeine), so it was on with the day. I had more than enough conferences to fill the afternoon and was armed with samples of work and ready by the time these parents came to see me. All of them showed up and other than a dry mouth and a sore jaw from talking for several hours, the afternoon went extremely well. I had parents whose comments and questions were constructive, they appeared to be appreciative of what their children were learning, and we parted on excellent terms. I left that afternoon hoping the remaining conferences would go as well. We're not always so lucky.

But that led me to thoughts of my position on the other side of the table when my kids were in third grade. You know, when I got to sit in the little kid chair while the teacher towered over me in the adult chair. He or she would show samples of my little prodigy's work and discuss issues such as behavior and study habits. When my kids were younger, I looked forward to these times despite the tiny plastic chairs that were not designed for adult behinds. I'm not a large woman, but mine spilled over the sides of plastic seat nonetheless. As my kids have gotten older, I look forward to these meetings with feelings similar to those I have before my annual mammogram. They are sometimes just as painful though the chairs are bigger.

Stuff happens and teachers (who have caffeine) are flexible by nature (if they have caffeine), so it was on with the day.

See, I know teacher-speak and what teachers say, (sorry parents) is not always exactly what we mean. For example, when I went to my 17 year old son's conferences this year, every one of the teachers began with the phrase, "Oh, Shawn is such a great kid!" This sounds good to those childless people or those whose children haven't gotten to high school yet. But I know what it really means; "It's a good thing he has such a good personality, because he doesn't do homework and is squeaking through by the skin of his teeth". I know my kid. He's a charmer all right, and he *IS* smart. But I also know the nature of the beast. Kids will get by if they can and let's face it, Senioritis is a real disease. But I take heart in the fact that it's not terminal if the teacher says, "He is such a great kid". Like I said, sitting on both sides has its advantages and so I thought I might share just a few phrases in teacher-speak to prepare you for your upcoming conference, and do a quick study for my seventh grader's conferences that are coming up.

1.) The teacher says," He's a little too chatty at times". Translation: "He talks so much that I'm afraid I'm thinking duct tape."

2.) The teacher says, "She's very social." Translation: "She's in the middle of every catty little girl fight on the playground."

Parent – Teacher Time
CONTINUED

3.) The teacher says, "She's working hard on paying attention". Translation: "She's busy with the lip gloss, necklace, cute-pie pencils and desk doo-dads that I wish you wouldn't buy her".

4.) The teacher says, "He's trying hard to stay in his seat". Translation: "I may have to seat belt him to his chair".

Alternatively, as a parent, I know there are things parents should never say to a teacher because I know how those translations go as well (guilty as charged I'm afraid). For example:

1.) The parent says "My son seems a little bored". Translation: "You are so boring I don't know how he sits here all day".

2.) The parent says, "I want her to be more challenged", Translation: "I don't feel like playing Barbie's when I get home from work, I want her to have something else to do but talk to me."

3.) The parent says "There's too much homework". Translation: "I never had this much homework when I was a kid."

4.) The parent says "How is he compared to the rest of the class?" Translation: "Should I brag or avoid the subject of school when I'm with other parents?"

So there you go, a few trade secrets from both sides. They may not be politically correct, but they are correct at least part of the time. It's tough at times to be in my position. ☉

Reporting on Report Cards

KATHY KENNEY-MARSHALL

My cell phone rang again on my way home. I've said it before, but I dread when the caller ID tells me that one of my children is calling me. This sounds strange because my children are the reason I gave in and bought a cell phone to begin with. But usually, calls from home bring some sort of drama that is best dealt with when I am not driving 65 mph on Rt. 128. This time, it was the happy sounding voice of my seventh grader calling to tell me that he got his report card. Being a good student, I expected nothing less than good, and judging from his tone, it was a beauty. "Guess what I got in English!" He said. "An A?" I responded, forgetting that middle schools grade with number averages instead of letter grades. "I got 100" He announced proudly. Wow. Nobody gets a perfect 100 percent as a final grade. I mean, I knew he was smart, but perfection? I was impressed. The fact that his conduct was only "fair" didn't bother me much. Imagine if he had behaved himself ... is there such a thing as 110 percent?

The rest of his card looked pretty darn good too as did my older son's, who is a senior. I was proud that evening and thought about the report cards I will not be sending home until January. They are three pages long and contain 76 items for assessment that must be rated using a number system devised, probably by the IRS or some other governmental bureaucracy. At the end of the report card, I get to write a narrative that will tell parents what all 76 of those items mean. It's great fun to fill out and certainly parents mark their calendars and take a personal day from work to figure them out. Of course in keeping with the logic of the document, parent teacher conferences occur before it goes home. I show the manuscript, I mean report card to parents, but when their eyes glaze over, I change the subject and pull out the student's writing journal to put them at ease. Yes, we still work on Reading and Writing and Arithmetic.

I remember report card day when I was a kid. Your teacher handed out those little orange clasped envelopes at the end of the day and you were either filled with gloom or skipped happily all the way home when you ran out of the building, hid behind the bushes and snuck a peek. In my house, the treat was chocolate pudding if you did exceptionally well. Average was not expected, so to me and my siblings, Cs did not exist until at least middle school when punishment was sure and swift when grades were below expectations. I'm not so sure how a parent would deal with the rating scale in place at many elementary schools today.

Usually there are numbers assigned to many items. The numbers range in some places from 1-4 or the letter N. N stands for, "Not evaluated yet." For example, in math (page three of report), a child might get a two under the topic "Gives probability of outcomes for simple situation". First the parent must figure out what constitutes a "simple situation", and then find the "Key to Progress" box back on page 1. Ah, there it is, a 2 means "Progressing with support". Hmmmm. Does that mean he can give the probability of the outcome for a simple situation, or does someone have to tell him what the word *probability* means, or perhaps, explain to the parent why a third grader has to have that skill when he can't add two digit numbers yet. And more important, does he get pudding or is his Play Station taken away on school nights? It's a dilemma.

Of course, the parent might miss the meaning of the number 2 mistaking it for the numbers 1, 2, and 3 that appear at the end of each section of the report card. In this case a 2 would mean "Satisfactory". Satisfactory is ok. Does that equate to a C like when we were in grade school? Upon further study, the parent might realize that those are the effort numbers. Or perhaps, the parent would see the "Key to Progress Box" on page three where the math item actually appears and mistake it for the 2 that means, "Needs to work more consistently on effort." That might be worthy of Play Station removal, maybe. Of course that "Key to Progress Box" is for Special Areas; in other words Gym, Art, and Music.

Yes, it's November and I'm already chomping at the bit to fill out these very informative reports. With only 24 students to report on this year, it should take me only 9 or 10 hours to fill in the 1,520 items. It took a little longer last year, but I have a head start this term ... I know what each "Key to Progress Box" applies to! In a world full of complicated life issues, it feels really good to have something uncomplicated and fun to look forward to. ◉

Report Cards Offer the Gift of Gab

KATHY KENNEY-MARSHALL

It's report time again in our town and I can usually ... no ... I can always tell what kind of report cards my children have gotten by the tone of their voices as they call me on my way home from work to give the oral report. Sometimes these calls are made to ellicit congratulations and secure the possibility of my stopping for a little treat on the way home. But sometimes the call is made to soften the blow. This term, I received no phone call from my seventh grader on report card day. I found this puzzling, because this was the student who got a 100 in English on his last report card. His grades are always worthy of praise, but a 100? Who earns a 100 in any subject, especially in the first term of middle school English? Apparently, my son does. Rewards are generally symbolic in my house as we don't subscribe to the notion that good grades warrant a paycheck. I know parents who offer monetary rewards for high marks, but my husband and I usually offer compensation in the way of a fast food from Burger King or McDonalds since those are never of the list of options when neither of us wants to cook.

When I got home that night, Mike met me with the report card and an avalanche of excuses and explanations before I had the front door closed. I took the dreaded document out of his hands and said as nicely as a parent could after a long day, "Stop talking and let me look". His 100 in English dropped to an 80 and his 94 in Spanish dropped to a 78. As I studied the remainder of the report card, I was pleased with all of his other subjects. Second term, I thought, is always a little harder and so this wasn't so bad. But looking at my son's face, I realized, it was. I was faced at that moment with what many call a "teachable moment". The issue I was faced with became how to respond to the precipitous drop in two subjects while recognizing the other good grades he had worked for. What I decided to do, was to place accountability where it belonged; on him. Though the look on his face spoke volumes about how he felt, I asked "What do you think of this?" Looking down at his suddenly fascinating feet, he responded, "I think it's fine." Feeling this untruth smack me in the face, I asked again. His answer this time was much more honest. He felt terrible about it. What ensued was a very open honest discussion about what was happening both with his class work and homework that would explain the decline. We were able to come up with a plan to help him and both of us left the discussion feeling relieved and satisfied.

Later that evening, as we sat playing a vocabulary match game (he won easily), I found myself wishing that all parenting moments could go as smoothly as this one. While I could have gotten on my high horse and ridden into the sunset, grounding him until the grades improved, I realized that nothing I could have said would have made him feel any worse about his waning grades in these two subjects. Not only that, both he and I realized that these are *HIS* grades after all, not mine, and not his dad's. I was glad it bothered him that he had not done his best. It showed that he felt ownership and control over his success or lack thereof and that he genuinely cared what Paul and I thought.

> *What I decided to do, was to place accountability where it belonged; on him. Though the look on his face spoke volumes about how he felt, I asked "What do you think of this?"*

As a parent, just as he is learning seventh grade English, we are learning how to be better parents. How we responded to his first "not so perfect" report card could have shut down communication if we simply berated his lack of achievement. Instead, we were able to open the door to a productive helpful discussion that made him feel supported, yet responsible. So as my son collected his 19 sets of matching Spanish vocabulary cards over my measly six, I humbly congratulated him and allowed him to gloat over his win, letting him think that his was the only victory of the night. In reality, we both won something bigger than report card grades; the open door to honest communication with each other. ◉

Third Grade Politics
KATHY KENNEY-MARSHALL

Though the polling booths have been packed up and put away, I am still thinking politics. But not the kind that most adults are thinking about. The hot topics; the war in Iraq, homeland security, the possibility of a draft, gay marriage, stem cell research, etc. are being hotly debated by the talk show pundits all around the radio dial. But my thoughts are centered here in my third grade classroom where I focus on the eight and nine year old children I teach. Of course, as all teachers do, I try to expose my class to important happenings in the world and so election time brought about a wonderful opportunity to do some real life teaching. Our school had a mock election planned for Tuesday, so while most of their parents were taking a few moments to enter a voting booth and exercise their right to vote, our little citizens were also lining up to cast their ballot for whomever their parents told them to vote for, or whomever their best friend was voting for.

Before Tuesday, however, I thought it might be fun to see what they did know about what was to happen in our country on November 2. While almost all of them knew that the presidential race was on, their ideas on politics gave me a few chuckles. For example, while none of them admitted that they thought political parties had anything to do with cake and funny hats, they weren't quite sure what they were. Finally one girl in my class raised her hand and said she thought there was something called a Republican party. "That's great." I said, "Does anyone know what the other major political party is?" At first all I got in response were blank stares, so I wrote the word *Republican* on the board. Suddenly a hand shot up in the back of the room. "George Bush is Republican!" stated a boy. "That's right, good for you!" I praised. Another hand, from a girl in the front who looked as though she might be experiencing a mild heart attack from the thought she was able to produce. "I know, I know the other party! The Dominicans!" she proudly called out. Oh boy, I had my work cut out for me. At least she got the right beginning letter. What followed was a lively discussion about third grade politics. We spent a morning of fact gathering starting with what they already thought they were experts on. Here's what they knew:

- Inauguration Day is when the new president moves into his office to live.
- The people who are fighting to be president are called candidates until Nov. 2
- George Bush comes from Taxes
- You vote where you are
- President Bush runs
- You vote by punching a hole or writing in pen, not pencil
- You can be a Dominican, a Republican, or a Liberal
- Every four years, there's an eviction
- John Kerry likes Heinz ketchup
- George Bush has more pets than John Kerry (one of the most important facts that brought forth 5 solid minutes of pet discussion.)
- If something happens to the President, the runner-up gets a turn

Of course, as all teachers do, I try to expose my class to important happenings in the world and so election time brought about a wonderful opportunity to do some real life teaching.

The election at our school didn't result in a win for George Bush like it did in the real election. Some children seemed quite put out by that. But the blow was softened a bit by the lingering high spirits over the Red Sox victory and a visit from former Red Sox player Lou Merloni who came to our school reading award assembly on Wednesday. Kids are like that, they bounce back easily and move on with the more important issues like real live baseball players at their school.

    I'm glad they knew something about elections, and hopefully after our lessons and activities they understand a little more about the process. However, when one child decided he would attend Electoral College after high school, I am relieved to know that these kids have 12 more years to learn about the process before they can cast their actual vote for the next president. ◉

A Turn for the Worse
KATHY KENNEY-MARSHALL

A neighbor recently brought over a paper entitled, "The Obituary of Common Sense." While entertaining, I had read it before several times in emails. Lately though, one particular sentence repeats itself in my head when I read my school email. The line says that "Common Sense took a turn for the worse when parents attacked teachers for doing the job that they themselves had failed to do in disciplining their unruly children." I find this to be all too common as my teaching career marks nearly a quarter of a century. This includes, but is not limited to expecting that kids do their homework. Recently for example a parent was incensed when her child was not given a sticker on a homework assignment that was not completed according to directions! A sticker!! It happened every once in a while when I was newer to the profession; a child on the verge of permanent punishment made up a story to "get me in trouble:" *"MOM!* The teacher is making me write every spelling word from the whole year 5,000 times each and it's May!" *"MOM!* She's making me write a 17 page paper on the 17 countries in West Africa ... by *TOMORROW!"* Most of the time, the parents of these ... embellishment makers, will write a note asking why I am torturing children, but for the most part, I get a very nice call or note letting me know about the tall tales that are coming home to deflect the attention off of themselves and whatever it is they have or haven't done, and onto me, the evil teacher in room B29!

As I spend more and more time in the classroom, I find myself addressing situations that make me believe that Common Sense is, if not dead, is rushing out the doors of many homes. Not too long ago, I had a parent call me to say that she was having trouble putting her child to bed. She asked what I could do to help her. I thought perhaps she dialed the wrong number and really meant to call the pediatrician. But sadly, I was mistaken. She literally asked me if I could come to her home to help her put her unruly-at-home son to bed because I didn't seem to have trouble with him at school. Another day,

I received a phone call from a distraught mother whose child was new to our school. She was upset because her very bright daughter wrote a very messy essay and reported, "Mrs. KKM said to do it this way." The mother berated me for forcing her child to do a bad job. It didn't take long to figure out the confusion; I asked the children to do a rough draft, but since they are only eight and I like to rhyme, I call it a "sloppy copy" and apparently I failed to explain the term properly to an

It happened every once in a while when I was newer to the profession; a child on the verge of permanent punishment made up a story to "get me in trouble:

appropriately literal third grader. The mother and I had a laugh and so did the student the next day. One of my favorites of late was a parent of a child who transferred from a very religious private school. The parent called to inquire about a discussion that her son relayed to her from the day. The conversation went something like this:

Parent: "Are you teaching about the family in school?"

Me: "No, there is a family/community unit in first grade, but not in third."

Parent: "Well are you teaching about alternative lifestyles?"

Me: (Now I was interested) "Hmm ... no. I can't figure out where you're going with this, why do you ask?"

Parent: "Mrs. Kenney-Marshall! We are a very conservative and religious family! Are you teaching homosexuality?!" (I almost choked on my water.)

What I wanted to say and almost did, but *MY* Common Sense took over just in time, "No, Ma'am, that's not until fourth grade." After a few more questions from me, I realized what she was talking about; in math class, I had talked about how certain numbers are related. For example; 4, 3, and 12 are related in multiplication and division. She was immensely relieved, but as I hung up the phone, I shook my head and found myself missing my good friend Common Sense who had apparently vacated her home that day. ☉

Liar, Liar, Pants on Fire

KATHY KENNEY-MARSHALL

As a classroom teacher, I am privy to many of the lies, most small, some outrageous that children tell. Esther comes to mind immediately as being the biggest repeat offender and governing champion of Legends in Lying. She brought it to an art form.

Esther was a beautiful girl, dark skinned, thin, five or six braids popping off her head each day with eyes that you could drown in. As the children lined up at the classroom door one morning, there was more excitement than is usual for a Tuesday. I was greeted with a chorus of, "Esther got bitten by a snake!" Esther stood back, looking at me expectantly. I asked her if this was true and she nodded, holding out her thumb that did indeed have two round puncture-type wounds on it. I looked it over and asked if she was ok, to which she nodded again, took her morning work, and quietly sat at her seat pretending to concentrate on the multiplication problem in front of her.

"When did this happen, Esther?" I asked her.

"Yesterday, after school", was her nonchalant answer.
It was a rainy spring and having had a sunny afternoon to play, I thought perhaps she found a snake outside and tried to catch it, end of story. I had learned throughout the year that Esther needed very little encouragement to stir up things in class, so I left well enough alone.

As we lined up for music class however, she asked to see the nurse because her snake bite hurt and she wanted a band-aid. I glanced at the injury and asked again about when it had occurred. She was off and running.

"It happened yesterday, at the zoo," she began. "My mother took me to the zoo and we went into the place where the snakes are and this man took out a snake to show us and when he put the snake away, he forgot to close the cage and the snake escaped! Everyone was looking for it all over the place, but I saw it and I just wanted to pet it but it bit me!"

She said all this in what appeared to be one breath. By this time, the horrified looks of her classmates spoke loudly, 'I'm not ever ever going to the snake house in the zoo again!' I had to continue the discussion because even I, a seasoned lie detector was having trouble with this one.

"Esther, where did you go to the zoo?"

"I dunno, some place in Boston."

"Ok, so your mother took you to the Franklin Park Zoo, and a snake actually escaped and bit you?"

"Yeah, see?" She held up her thumb to show me once again.

"So what happened then?"

"The man put the snake back in the cage and remembered to lock it in this time," she answered somberly.

"No, Esther, what happened to you? Didn't you go to a Dr.?"

"Oh yeah! My mother had to bring me to the Dr. and it hurt. I even cried. I cried a lot!"

"Go to the nurse, Esther, and make sure you tell her all about it." I instructed.

I brought the class to the music room and then went to speak to the school nurse.

"So, what do you think of our snake bite victim?" I asked, knowing that Nurse Judy would get the truth out of her immediately. She looked over the tops of her glasses and rolled her eyes saying that it was a simple fall off of a bike that caused the "snake bite."

After telling the class that she had lied and after calling her mom, (who roared with laughter), I convinced the rest of the children that it was indeed safe to go to the zoo again. I wanted to tell them that it's safer to handle a snake than to believe a word Esther said, but that seemed neither kind nor professional. Hopefully at this writing, she has curbed her enthusiasm for the economy of truth telling, or perhaps, she just may end up using her fine honed skill into a way to make a living for herself one day as a novelist, (though I swear this is a true story).

Not all lies are so big in third grade. But some do warrant the clever intervention of a teacher with a little ingenuity. Somehow, children in third grade think that if they get away with a fib, it never really happened. One day, I got them to think otherwise and I admit, in order to do this, I lied.

> *Not all lies are so big in third grade. But some do warrant the clever intervention of a teacher with a little ingenuity.*

Liar, Liar, Pants on Fire

After lunch my group was following another third grade class up the two sets of stairs to our classrooms. Someone from the higher staircase decided to rid his palate of the pancake on a stick he had the good fortune to have been served for lunch. The "loogie" missed my hand by mere centimeters. In a fit of panic … or was it annoyance, I yelled, *"EWWWWW! STOP! Everyone STOP!"* Miss Y, the teacher of the perpetrator looked surprised as did all of the children. When I explained the reason for my outburst, Miss Y was visibly upset.

"Who did this?" she demanded. Now think about it; if you were eight or nine, faced with 50 peers and two angry teachers, would you confess? Certainly not. But I had a plan. I told Miss Y that when we got back to our rooms, I wanted her to hand out little pieces of paper so that the culprit could plead guilty anonymously. This I hoped would offer a little assurance that the dirty deed would remain between me and him. But, that wasn't assurance enough for me. I threw down my winning card.

"Miss Y, if nobody owns up to their actions, I will be forced to take out my DNA kit."

I think I noticed Miss Y, a much younger though excellent teacher bite the insides of her cheeks to stop herself from laughing. I remained serious and put on my best third grade scary teacher look. Never before or since has there been such a quiet line of children in the halls of our elementary school as the guilty and innocent worried about this very mysterious but frightening DNA kit in my possession.

Though the frantic whispers in Miss Y's class held promise for a speedy resolution to what has become known as the "Loogie Incident", nobody confessed, even in anonymity. I had to tell yet another lie when the children asked if I had found the perpetrator of such a gross crime. I informed them that the custodian had wiped away the evidence with bleach and with it all hopes of a DNA sample. But, I admonished, that person knows what he or she did and I certainly hoped he or she had learned from this close call with the principal. I think I learned more that day; even eight year olds are savvy enough to call a teacher's bluff.

Thankfully, the custodian never ratted me out because the DNA kit, an old science kit with real glass test tubes sits gathering dust in my closet just in case I'm almost hit with another expectorant. Sadly, pancake on a stick is still on the school menu, so I may need it yet. ◉

Just Plain CRUMBS

Electronically Challenged?

KATHY KENNEY-MARSHALL

We got a new 48 inch high definition, (high def for you electronic geeks) television recently. Recently as in last spring. It's ok I suppose if you like television ... which I do, sort of. I mean, I look forward to certain shows each week, *Survivor* (again, I'll admit to *Survivor* fanaticism), *House, Desperate Housewives,* and *Grey's Anatomy,* but I can honestly say that I watch far less television than the average American. Which is why, when I came home on a Tuesday night from the gym with a rare two hours to myself, I decided that a glass of chardonnay, candle aroma wafting through the living room, and the decadence of a chick flick sounded like heaven.

I showered, put on ugly yet comfy sweatpants, heated the homemade chicken soup I made the night before, and actually felt a little giddy over my lazy plans for the evening. Everything was perfect ... until I realized I couldn't figure out how to turn on the television.

Apparently, while I wasn't looking, the "ON" button on the remote had been rendered obsolete. There are more buttons on the remote than I have pairs of shoes (Carrie Bradshaw would understand this ... Did I mention I love Sex in the City too?). Being as clever as I am, when I saw the second remote that had almost made its getaway to the abyss of under-the-sofa-land, I thought I had solved the problem. I must have had to push the ON button on that one too. It didn't work.

But my error was not as bad as it appeared when I noticed that one of the remotes had the word "TV" on it. All I had to do was push that button simultaneously with the ON buttons of both remotes. Wrong again. So I tried the AUX button, the VCR button, (we don't own a VCR anymore, but it was worth a try), the ANT button, though I'm not sure what ants have to do with television, and finally I threw the remote across the room. Luckily, it landed on a comfy chair and didn't break.

Then I saw the true culprit; The Play Station. My thirteen year old must have been playing a video game before he left and forgot to reset the TV. I thought about calling him ... but then remembered that he didn't have a cell phone. I thought also about calling my husband who was at a Parent Meeting which would have been entirely inappropriate and dangerous to the longevity of my marriage. In desperation, I called the cable company.

> *I decided that television wasn't really worth the rise in my blood pressure so I picked up a book and began to read until my son came home and I pounced*

Stan answered with a very polite, "What can I help you with tonight?"

To which I responded, "I'll tell you, but you have to promise not to laugh."

He laughed. I hung up after making sure that he was still breathing.

I decided that television wasn't really worth the rise in my blood pressure so I picked up a book and began to read until my son came home and I pounced. " Fix that television or the Playstation gets thrown into oncoming traffic!" I screamed along with several unkind expletives that no 13-year-old should hear from his own mother. He hadn't been playing video games. My bad.

I had to call the cable company again and pray that Stan, who I called many unflattering names, didn't answer. A lovely woman answered and walked me through a process.

"Do you have a DVR?" she asked.

"Huh?" I responded with as much intelligence as I could.

"You have three boxes, correct?" she patiently continued.

"I only see one." I answered

"Ok, dear, let's start here ... .what does your cable box say?"

"It isn't making any sound." I said, "That's part of the problem."

I heard her sigh, blow her nose ... or was that a laugh? Finally, through the magic of technology, she had my television turned on complete with both sound and picture. But by then, it was way past my bedtime and I didn't feel like watching television any longer. Also by then, I had unplugged the DVD player, the Play Station, and probably 60 out of the 70 cords behind the TV. My husband insists there are only six, but I have the dust bunnies in my hair that prove otherwise.

Choices Aren't Always That Easy

KATHY KENNEY-MARSHALL

We recently visited our son in Florida where he is a freshman at FAU. He does not love the experience, but a visit from home sometimes calms the soul. Of course a visit from the entire family, an experience that is almost foreign for modern human beings who happen to be teenagers, (or the parents of said teens), can be stressful by the twelvth hour of blissful togetherness. Still, we made the most of our time by going to a Japanese restaurant that he loves. The five of us, along with John, a good friend from home studied the menu. The conversation started out like this;

"You want a salad, Shawn?"

"No, I don't like the Japanese salad dressing"

Then the waiter came to take our order.

"Would you like the miso soup or the salad?" he asked our son.

"I'll have the salad, please." He answered politely. The waiter finished taking orders and left.

"I thought you didn't like the salad," I asked.

"I don't" he replied, "but I HATE the soup."

This was worthy of a few chuckles at the dinner table perhaps, but it got me thinking about choices. Sometimes it's as simple as soup or salad when you actually like both. But sometimes, like in the case of my son, it's all about the lesser of two evils. Though he could have chosen neither, some choices in life aren't as palatable as the ones he was offered and you have to choose one over the other.

I think immediately of a phone call I received from my dad's sister after a really long week. My aunt almost never calls me. I am the caller. It's my role and it's fine with me. I usually find myself lost in the 'catching up' time that brings with it good feelings and a hefty phone bill. So on a Friday night when I walked through the door and actually got the message from my youngest, a miracle in itself in that messages seem to disappear into a black hole when given to one of your offspring, I knew it couldn't be good. It wasn't.

Seven years ago, my father died of esophageal cancer just after he turned 62. He was diagnosed in November and died on May 1. It was the worst six months of all of our lives. Cancer of the esophagus is particularly cruel. At the time, the doctors warned us not to read about it on the Internet. I listened to them for a year, then I read. I finally understood their warning. There were no survival rates and my father became another statistic. It was a painful time full of lousy choices for him; chemotherapy and radiation first or surgery? A food tube two days before Thanksgiving because the mass was discovered so late or a possible last turkey dinner, leaving the tumor to grow an extra few days? Soup or salad?

There were six months worth of lousy choices for us; should we let the kids see him in his decline against his wishes? Should we visit every day or every weekend? Soup or salad?

The doctors called us on a few different occasions toward the end. We had to decide about treatments for him when he could no longer make decisions. As a family, we had to decide when it was time to call it quits. It was when his kidneys failed we all agreed. But when that time came, it was too hard to make that final decision. Soup or salad? I'll take the soup ... no the salad ... no the soup. In the end it didn't matter, he died anyway. No soup, no salad.

So this phone call from his only sibling came with ironic bad news. Her husband, my dad's best friend, was diagnosed with cancer of the esophagus. Ironic because it is the same disease that took my father, and because it is not so common a form of cancer, yet here it was in our family again.

His is in the early stages and there have been many advances since my father's rather late stage diagnosis. My aunt had optimism in her voice as she told me that there was a good chance he'd beat it, as long as he chose treatment over doing nothing. Soup or salad? Choices. It seems that there are so many in our lives that are not so important and yet we agonize over them. But in the end, maybe it's just important to know that there ARE choices even though none are appealing. Soup or salad?

Maybe Shawn had it right during that dinner. Make your choices while you can because sometimes life has a way of taking them from you, leaving you hungry for just a little more. ◉

Finding Your Inner Child at Christmas

KATHY KENNEY-MARSHALL

There is something about Christmas that makes me feel like I'm a kid again. Perhaps it's the colors of the season or the decorations that materialize around Halloween. Maybe excitement is as contagious as the common cold so the children in my classroom infect me with enthusiasm for candy canes and tinsel. Or possibly it is the memories of childhood that emerge from the spaces in my brain where they've been hiding for 11 months. This year I found myself reminiscing about Auntie Carolyn's silver aluminum Christmas tree. When I was small it seemed so fancy and modern. It changed colors with an oscillator that flashed red, green, yellow, and blue hues onto the fake stilted branches. When that tree came out of the attic, it surely meant Christmas would soon follow. Though I loved her flashy tree, I knew even then that I wouldn't want one in our house. Picking out the tree was a family adventure, but more than that, I loved the way a fresh tree brought the smell of Christmas into our house.

We'd hang the ornaments on it and fight over who got to put up certain special ones, like the crooked old wax soldiers whose hooked heads were reattached several times with an old Bic lighter leaving them neck-less and singed, but adored anyway. I especially loved the elves who sat cross-legged and whose faces always looked like they hadn't a care in the world. These memories, though far past, remain part of what I cherish about Christmas; the traditions I counted on and thought would remain the same forever.

Erma Bombeck said, "There's nothing sadder in this world than to awake Christmas morning and not be a child." I remember that Christmas too. It was just my father and me picking out a tree in the nearly empty lot just days before Christmas. With a divorce in progress and my siblings living elsewhere, we decided that we should choose a tree that needed lonely us. We found one and asked the attendant how much he'd give us to take it off his hands. He laughed and charged $5.00 for the stick that we loaded on top of the car and hauled home.

As we put it in the tree stand, we stood back and shook our heads. It truly was a Charlie Brown Christmas tree. The scrawny trunk held sparse branches that might not withstand the weight of some of the old ornaments and certainly not the wax soldiers. We did the best we could and told ourselves that it was beautiful.

It was then that I realized there was a magic in childhood Christmases that I was losing. It was rather like the story of *The Polar Express* and the first gift of Christmas. I was losing my ability to hear the magic of the season and it was sad. What I didn't know then was that I didn't have to lose my childhood; I could pull out the memories or even better, add new ones. And so our emaciated tree that year found its way into the cherished stories of Christmases past.

Having children made Christmas come alive again with a passion I never thought possible. It was in the delighted faces of my children as we put lights on the tree. It was their eyes when we hung stockings or took a drive in the car to look at lights. It was the simplicity of making cupcakes for their classmates at school. And most of all, it was the home made cards with words misspelled and smudgy Magic Marker drawings. My husband and I have tried to make Christmas as wonderful and magical for our children as our parents had done for us. This I've found is the greatest gift of all.

And so as I wake this year on Christmas morning, with nearly grown children, I am not sad because I am not a child. I will, as always, wake up the child inside and look at our holiday as I did when I was nine. I will marvel at the wonder the season invites us to make memorable and I will hear the magic of Christmas.

Wake up the child inside of you this year. I'd love to know what you'll find. ☉

Getting the Hang of Hanging Out on the Curb

KATHY KENNEY-MARSHALL

I was never one to hang out on the curb when I was a teen. You know, I never quite fit in with the cooler kids who just looked natural hanging out in their cool jeans, smoking cigarettes, swearing or telling jokes that I wouldn't have understood anyway. Also, my mother didn't let me wear jeans or smoke cigarettes, and I was way too uncool to try. I wasn't exactly a nerd in high school, or a jock, or ... anything really. I was just kind of there. I did what I was supposed to do some of the time, got relatively good grades, most of the time, and didn't cause too many grays to sprout prematurely from my parents' hair follicles. In other words, I was pretty boring.

So when my three kids were finally too big to fit in the back seat of my Escort, (station wagon of course), I was actually excited to join the growing ranks of Americans who bought a mini-van. It was a respectable vehicle that no policeman would ever pull over for drag racing down the main street of town on a Saturday night. If a "soccer-mom-type" is going too fast down said street, it is obviously because she has an emergency with one of her children. An unfair advantage for sure, but one small perk for being responsible at all other times seemed like a fair trade off. Anyway, this role of dependable mom was an easy transition for someone like me who would remain in my familiar identity, (boring), for at least part of my adult life.

As is always the case however, my kids and their friends got too old for the town soccer team, graduated out of Little League, and got their licenses needing fewer and fewer carpool rides from me. It was time to buy a new car.

I thought about it for a long time and decided that I was not ready for anything as cool as a Mustang, (even though I really wanted one), and I was not old enough for a Cadillac or a Grand Marquee, at least I hoped. So I stuck to my practical way of thinking and went shopping for a Honda. We'd owned a couple of used ones before and they seemed to live forever. They're also pretty good looking so I allowed myself the shallowness of character to look for a used Accord that was also cute. Cute was as far into the threat of mid-life crisis as I was willing to go.

That is, until I found, "The Batmobile."
The Batmobile, as it was called by the dealership from which I bought it was more than cute. It was black and sporty. The two-tone gray leather heated seats were exquisite. It had a sunroof/moon roof *AND* a bug shield! It had a spoiler on the back and some off-market tail lights that screamed mid-life crisis ... or cool, I'm still not sure which. But it didn't matter because it was love at first sight – for me anyway, I can't speak for the car though I think it was fond of me as well.) I bought it after having the dual exhaust removed for fear of noise pollution in my neighborhood, and I also had them removed the "skirt" and the small fire extinguisher on the front dashboard. I wanted to be cool, but not *THAT* cool.

> *I felt so uncool all of a sudden with my car hanging there. He told me not to try to move the car and asked me to come in to his mini-mart where it was warm.*

Just this morning however, only three weeks into Honda-Cooler-Than-A-Mother-Is-Allowed-To-Be-Ownership, I decided to finally hang out on the curb. Unfortunately it wasn't with the cool kids, (or moms.) Also unfortunately, I couldn't get off the curb. After getting gas before work, I made a serious misjudgement. What looked from my viewpoint, (and mid-life vision), like a three-inch edging of cement, was actually a drop of two feet on the other side to the sidewalk below. As I was pulling out of the gas station into very busy morning traffic, I miscalculated my distance from the edging and literally got stuck – my new car was hanging off the curb, its passenger side tire several inches off the ground.

The owner of the station, a very nice man named Nick, came running out to see if I was OK. I was definitely *NOT*. I felt so uncool all of a sudden with my car hanging there. He told me not to try to move the car and asked me to come in to his mini-mart where it was warm. He informed me that I was the sixth person in only two weeks to get caught up in the same spot. Ok, now I was only slightly stupid ... at least I had company. I only hoped that the other five weren't 95 or drunk!

Getting the Hang of Hanging Out on the Curb

Nick called a tow truck company to come rescue my new love and me. As I waited though, with a cup of coffee that Nick graciously poured for me, the most amazing things started happening.

A police officer stopped to see if he could help. And older gentleman buying gas offered his advice stating that if I had front wheel drive I could do this on my own. He was wrong, but he walked out to the car and we gave it a try anyway. He wished me luck and went on his way. A young woman walked over and commiserated a similar experience she had and said she hoped my day ended better than it began. At one point, a very muscular looking fellow walked in and gathered several customers and they tried to life my car off the curb. While that didn't work either, I was touched that they took the time. Nick, in the meantime, talked to me about my work and about the others who ended up in the same spot I was in. No, they weren't the elderly or the intoxicated. I felt a bit better. He complained about the curb being a hazard that he had been trying to rectify for months.

When the tow truck finally arrived and rescued me, I thanked Nick profusely for helping to turn a lousy situation into one that showed me a better side of human kind. So many people approached me just talk or offer help. It was refreshing. It made me think that maybe I ought to hang out on the curb more often! ◉

Going Back to School: A Big Deal at Any Age

KATHY KENNEY-MARSHALL

Like a colleague of mine, I decided to enroll in a creative writing class this summer. I wanted to broaden my horizons, try something different, see a new perspective in my writing. In other words, I had a voucher to take a class at Framingham State College for having a student teacher last semester.

I found a class that meets three nights a week for a bit over three hours. Add the hour and a half drive time during rush hour traffic to get there and the 45 minute ride home at a time I would normally be snuggled in my pjs with a good book, and that totals just over 15 hours a week for five weeks. I can do that! But then there's that pesky homework. Add another couple of hours and I can still do it though this was beginning to feel a little more worrisome. I thought about it, weighed the options, and signed up anyway.

The first class met on a Wednesday. I was nervous, as I suppose lots of "kids" are on the first day of class. Lesson #1; I understand the first day jitters that my students experience. See! I'm learning already! As I walked in, just five minutes early, (fashionably late would not be acceptable in school), I realized quickly that I could be the mother, or at the very least the aunt to most of the other students. That's OK, I thought, you're never too old to learn.

I found a seat woefully close to the front of the room, (Lesson #2, five minutes early is still late if you want a seat in the back), and I started a grocery list. One point for age. I would use my time wisely while waiting for the professor. Time ticked away and my grocery list got longer until finally, I realized that I would have enough food to feed the state of Rhode Island. He finally did arrive, 24 hours later. (No, I did not stay and continue my list.)

The second first night jitters didn't dissipate as he began to hand out reams of papers including a syllabus that was written in Greek ... I think. He'll explain I thought and anyway, I was not the oldest in the class any longer. I sat back and listened. This was to be a blackboard class, he announced. Oh good, I thought, he'll write on the board a lot, something I am quite familiar with. I began to relax. Until he mentioned the words *laptop* and *website.* Huh?

Apparently something devious had been going on in higher education while I wasn't paying attention. Computers were not something I would go home and do my assignments on any longer. I was supposed to bring a laptop to class. I didn't have a laptop. I barely have a lap! I felt panic increasing as I then realized that he wasn't in fact going to write on the blackboard at all. Blackboard is some kind of newfangled way of "posting" homework electronically. How could I have missed the obvious clue that there wasn't a piece of chalk or a big black felt eraser anywhere? Lesson #3; teachers are really sneaky, my third graders were right!

After making it through the explanation of the first assignment, sort of, we launched into poetry. Finally! Something I wasn't having palpitations about. I began to feel more at home. We hadn't yet written a word in the Creative Writing class, but I was enjoying the discussion even if it was only about as lively as the first day of third grade when the kids are still afraid of me ... I mean apprehensive about my expectations.

Finally, the underhandedness of the teaching profession reared its ugly head again as all but five of us were dismissed. We were asked about our graduate project since this was also a class offered to undergrads. Project? Had I been working on another shopping list when he mentioned a project? In two minutes or less I had to produce an idea for a novel and have said novel written in five weeks? Apparently my anxiety caused temporary deafness. It was really simple. I merely had to think of an idea for a project that would increase my workload tenfold in order to bring my credits up to graduate level standards. Simple. Lesson #4; nothing is simple.

By the time you read this, I will have probably almost finished this course.* I will probably be thankful that I took it and I will probably look back on the terrifying beginnings and think, "what was the big deal?" Lesson #5, graduate level writing classes ARE a big deal even if you are a writer. I'll tell you if I passed ... on second thought, maybe I won't

*I'm happy to report, as of the publication of this book, I indeed finished that course and several others. I not only passed, but passed with a 4.0. Being a perfectionist has its advantages! And I am now the proud owner of a laptop, and sadly, a lap. ☉

To Gossip or Not to Gossip, a Pop-Culture Conundrum

KATHY KENNEY-MARSHALL

Seinfeld is a contemporary classic show. Its popularity is astounding. In my family, we own the boxed DVD set including the table ornaments from Monk's Café where Elaine orders "really big salads" and George and Jerry talk about nothing. Sometimes I need a little nothing in my life. But is this show about nothing? I recently found myself in a *Seinfeld* situation and began to wonder about how much 'nothing' can become 'something' if we let it.

For example, I ran into an acquaintance at the gym who I hadn't seen for a while. This woman, though I've always liked her, isn't someone with whom I am close. We bump into each other at the grocery store once in a while and have pleasant interactions about our kids, but that's about the extent of our relationship. So that morning as we said hello, I was shocked when she proceeded to tell me, in vivid detail about her impending divorce. She gave me information from soup to nuts and everything in between. I'm not sure she took a breath as the tumult of her life came spilling out. I felt terrible for her, and more than a little puzzled. I guess I was in the wrong place (for me), at the right time, (for her). She needed to unload and I was a familiar face. As she began feeling lighter after her tirade, I was left holding a heavy bag of unwanted information. I knew, for instance, that her husband is being served divorce papers next week. He doesn't even know this. I knew his eating, drinking, and sleeping habits, along with other behaviors I can't discuss here. Suffice to say, when she walked away, 20 valuable gym minutes later, I knew more than I ever needed to know and then a little extra. To make matters worse, she asked that I not tell anyone except Lisa and Ann Marie, two mutual friends. "Yes", she said, "you can tell them." Going back to my *Seinfeld*-moment, I wanted to scowl while sneering the word, "Jerry!".

Remember the episode? Jerry is bothered by an acquaintance who asks him to say "hi" to Elaine. He whines about it throughout the show. "Why can't he say hi himself? Am I now obligated to say hi? When he sees Elaine again, he'll want to know if I said "hi". If I don't pass on the 'hi', will he be angry? Why is it my responsibility to say 'hi'?" All of these points seemed mildly entertaining on a television show, but I never gave it much serious thought until at the gym that morning.

Not a fan of idle gossip, or juicy gossip for that matter, I felt stuck. Was I now obligated to pass this information on to Lisa and Ann Marie? In doing so, was I gossiping, or honoring someone's request? If I didn't pass on the divorce story, would this woman feel that her life's horrid ordeal didn't warrant some sort of discussion? The issue felt heavy as I stepped on the elliptical and began my workout. I became agitated at the responsibility of my unwelcome position. This indeed was a *Seinfeld*-esque moment.

To tell or not to tell, a very intriguing place to find myself. I was having dinner with Lisa that evening so I had to decide. Throughout the day, I changed my mind several times.

I thought, "I'll tell her". But realizing that our whole dinner might be ruined by the unpleasant business of a messy sad divorce, I changed my mind.

"I'm not telling." But if I don't tell, what happens next time I run into this woman and she asks if I told.

"I'll definitely tell", I concluded. Then another big fat "but" came to mind. Perhaps this woman didn't really want me to tell anyone until after the papers were served.

I definitely wasn't telling. This time, I wouldn't change my mind ... until 7:30 when we got to the restaurant and Lisa said hi. "Hi," I said, "Did you hear about So-and-So?" The gossip filter in my brain had vanished and I was telling the story faster than I could reconnect with my strict no gossip rule that resided in it. It didn't matter after all because Lisa already knew. Ann Marie told her. She heard in aisle 7 of the supermarket. I wondered why nobody told me! — !

So in the end, it didn't matter. And what I've decided is that gossip, whether good or bad, permitted or prohibited is something that I cannot spend so much time worrying about. And in a *Seinfeld* world where problems about 'nothing' are solved in 23.5 minutes, that's about all the time we need to give them in real life. And even that may be too long. ◉

Grampa Joe
KATHY KENNEY-MARSHALL

When I was very young, my Italian grandfather had magnificent family cookouts in the summer. I remember that we stayed for a very long time and there was always delicious food to eat. He made his own sausage and meat pies. He grilled and roasted peppers while my grandmother tended the pasta and gravy. After hours of eating, Grampa Joe and the Italian uncles played 45s. This was a card game that required lots of yelling after having had so much food and homemade wine that they drank from jelly glasses. Sometimes, my sister and I fell asleep on his enormous bed and my parents would carry us to the car to go home.

When I was eight, I had a white rabbit named Harvey. He was big and cantankerous for a bunny. He sometimes bit me and he always rubbed the fur off his nose on the bowl in his cage. He was not a typical rabbit, but I loved him. When Grampa Joe came over on summer Sunday afternoons, he delighted in picking Harvey up by his ears and saying what a good rabbit soup he could make out of him. I cried every time.

When I was nine, Grampa Joe and Gramma Rita rented a house on the beach. They came to pick me and my sister up to take us to spend time with our cousins. Our parents would join us later in the week. It was the first time I slept away from my parents for more than a night. I cried then too. But Grampa Joe made me sandwiches of egg and Italian gravy with onions. He brought Tripoli's pizza and pastries. He played the game meant for babies, "I've got your nose!" And I laughed even though I was too big for baby games.

When I was a teenager, Grampa Joe came to take care of our three dogs while we were on vacation. One of the dogs bit him as he entered our dark house one night. I felt really bad, but Grampa thought it showed what good watch dogs they were.

In my adulthood, Grampa Joe started to look older and smaller. But he still made sausages with his thick Italian hands. I watched those hands push seasoned pork into growing sausage casings without ever breaking the fragile membranes.

I saw my strong Grampa cry for the first time when Gramma Rita died. Broken-hearted I watched, crying for him and the loss of his love.

I didn't visit very often, because I had children, a job and not enough time. At least that's what I told myself. And when I did manage a visit, it made me sad to see him sitting in his kitchen rocking chair where a ragged yellow toy bird hung from a spring on the ceiling. There was so much to learn from and about him if only I made the time.

Paul and I took him out one day and spent hours listening to him tell life stories. As a teen he traveled from his home in Lawrence, MA to New York in the early 1900's. He slept in the park until he and his buddy got a job in a factory. When they could afford it, they rented a small unfurnished apartment. They slept on the floor but it was better than the park in a rainstorm. When they could afford it they bought furniture, piece by piece. There weren't credit cards back then, but it didn't matter because he wouldn't have used one.

He worked hard and earned an apprenticeship as a machinist, a job he did for the rest of his life. He returned to Lawrence and married Josephine. He had two daughters; my Auntie Marilyn and my mother. When Mom was only three or four, Josephine died of TB. Grampa Joe left his daughters with his parents who spoke no English. Auntie Marilyn and my young mother, Rosalind learned to speak Italian on their farm in Methuen while he traveled to California. He came back, remarried, and had my Aunt Kathy and Uncle Vinnie.

He told us these tales over lunch and I swore that day that I would go to him with a tape recorder and record his life on paper. Except that life got in the way.

Grampa Joe died recently and his stories are buried with him. Now I must try to bury my regret at having lost Grampa Joe and the wonderful words that were woven into his oral history.

A third grade poet once wrote; In life, there is no turning back, but still, sailing through the sky with your Nana is a possibility in your heart."

I will sail with Grampa Joe in mine and hold close a few chapters of his life story. I know we are never too old to learn, and perhaps Grampa's lesson is to remember to take the time to listen before it's too late.

Gym Etiquette

KATHY KENNEY-MARSHALL

It was a fight during class. The police had to be called and the result was chaotic. It started with a scowl that communicated vile thoughts. Several whispered insults were uttered and a few slurs were slung leading to louder abusive commentary. Next there was water involvement that ruined a new hairdo and made mascara run. Then an all out brawl ensued. The teacher tried to intervene unsuccessfully. They should have been sent to the principal's office except that they were taking the class at a gym. It was not a kickboxing class or even aerobics. The melee occurred during yoga.

The peaceful feelings guaranteed by posing as a downward dog, upward cat, or pooping platypus don't prevail when unwritten but well known rules are broken. There are policies posted at the front desk of the gym I frequent. But these regulations seem pointless. For example: no open toed shoes allowed while working out. Well, duh. If you need this rule to be written down then you also deserve to have a 20 pound dumbbell dropped on your toes. Only a human dumbbell would wear sandals or flip flops to work out.

Another stupid rule states that grunting is forbidden. I don't mind the grunting so much unless of course it is accompanied by the passing of gas while lifting a barbell. If you are straining so hard that all bodily gasses escape, it's obvious to me that the weight is simply too heavy.

The unwritten rules are common courtesies that gym frequenters just know by instinct. Gym Etiquette for new members should be made mandatory when signing away your life (or your bank account) upon joining. I would happily teach it for a small fee. My curriculum would address many of the problems that arise in any exercise establishment and would alleviate all visits from the police. I envision a program that will highlight but not be limited to these four lessons;

Lesson 1: Sweat; what to do with it. Everybody sweats while running on a treadmill or hiking a stair master. After you have finished using any of the cardiovascular equipment, it must be sterilized using the mystery blue water in the squirt bottles littering the floor of the gym. Clean rags should be used to wipe the machine unless you can't find one in which case you may use a dirty one. And if you don't sweat, you're probably there to pick up a date for Saturday night and should pretend to clean the machine anyway. In the event that there are no spray bottles filled with blue stuff, spit is not allowed as a cleaning agent.

Lesson 2: Farting and other bodily emissions; how to get away with it. Since they are not allowed in the gym, it is most difficult to blame the dog when you pass gas. During an aerobics class if you find that you're gassy due to whatever you ingested before you arrived, it might serve you well to find some waste left on the sidewalk from an inconsiderate pet owner. That way, you can still use the dog excuse. You will be asked by the management to clean the offending sneaker, but by then, the damage is done. If you are on the weight room floor, see above suggestion and use lighter weights.

Lesson 3: Spots in the aerobic room: dos and don'ts. Loyal gym members, a.k.a. fanatics, have a certain area they occupy for every class. If you take that 'spot', be prepared to be crowded out and looked at in menacing ways from the "regulars." Be especially careful during kickboxing classes as a wayward hook or sidekick may find its way millimeters from your face. To avoid this intimidation, wait until the class is full and take any available floor space next to another frightened newbie who doesn't yet have a reserved space.

Lesson 4: Mats; how close is too close? During Pilates, Yoga, or even at the end of an aerobic class, mats are used. When placing your mat, (usually drenched with sweat from the last class), make sure you can stretch your arms out without touching the person on any side of you. If you see a mat that has been placed too close to you while you were in the bathroom to avoid a tough exercise, don't move it! It is the mat user's responsibility to reposition unless of course, it is a gym regular in which case your best strategy is to vacate the area immediately, (this was the cause of the above mentioned combat).

These are just a few of the lessons that should be taught during gym orientation. There are more of course, but some things should be learned by experience. Now, I must go reserve my spot for "Bikini Bodies by Babs". There's a 22-year-old whose body is already bikini ready and she's been inching toward my spot. She apparently, missed Lesson 3. ◉

Living Well through Chemistry
KATHY KENNEY-MARSHALL

Having had my share of health issues over the past several years, and probably the shares of half of the population of Massachusetts, I have been changed in ways that healthy people can never understand. I have become more in tune with my body and have increased my vocabulary tenfold. Most of these words have to do with parts of the body. Of course, my favorite body part name is the uvula. After my last surgery, I suffered from a sore throat after being intubated for several hours.

Intubated, for those who don't watch *ER, House, Nip Tuck,* or any of the other wonderfully realistic medical dramas on TV, means that the anesthesiologist (doc that makes you let the other doc with the sharp object do whatever she wants), shoves a tube down your throat so you will breath during surgery. Breathing while on the operating table is not an option like say, singing Christmas Carols.

When I told the nurse about my sore throat, she called the anesthesiologist who asked her to see if he had bruised my uvula. A bruised uvula is not as pleasant as a hematoma on the patella (bruise on the kneecap). As soon as she told me what she had to check for I opened my mouth immediately since the uvula is that little doohickey that hangs down the back of your throat (obviously). And though I am a little smarter for my troubles, I must say that I have not come out of these medical maladies completely educated to the after-care of surgery.

Sometimes you go home, take pain medication and watch shows that make you think you had a lobotomy instead of whatever it is you had done. But sometimes, the job of healing is more complicated than figuring out a rebate form.

I am currently on a myriad of medications that are supposed to help nurse back to health (if they don't kill me first). To help my body survive these meds, my acupuncturist has given me several herbal supplements. My house is beginning to look like a pharmacy. My refrigerator is full of herbs, my cabinets are brimming with healing teas, and the bathroom cabinet is a study in phonics with the unusual names for the pills inside.

I have the bottles lined up on the bathroom shelf in alphabetical order to help keep them straight. The sheer number of the bottles take up one and a half shelves. That is not the problem. The problem lies in how and when they are taken. For example, three of the medications must be taken twice a day with or without food. That's easy, one in the morning and one in the evening. Another one orders one to two pills every three to four hours. So in a drug induced haze, I must decide how many of these to take and when. There are another two that should be taken every six hours with food. I must also drink eight ounces of water immediately with certain pills which makes me wonder if that means eight ounce per pill or per dose. Having to take two pills, this might mean chugging 16 ounces of water which may cause me to vomit leaving my stomach empty; which would help with certain medications but not with others.

I tried making a chart but I fell asleep through two of the dosages leaving me confused as to which to make up and when. Then I put all of the doses in little medicine cups like Nurse Ratchet used in *One Flew Over the Cuckoo's Nest* and lined them up on the kitchen counter. I did manage to stay awake for all of them except then I knocked over three of the cups. Since several of the pills look alike and I had already taken narcotics, I didn't trust myself to separate them accurately. I waited until my husband came home an hour later to decipher them. When I finally found a system that worked the Doctor's office called and added a glitch to this medication mayhem. I have an infection that requires that I ditch one med (the easy one taken at night before bed), to one that I must take every six hours on an empty stomach. I'm not panicking, but I am trying to figure out a way to eat that leaves my stomach still empty. I will get through all this I know ... though for the life of me, I'm not sure how to add this latest pill to my system. Any email tips from experienced medication moguls would be greatly appreciated. ◉

Reality Television Hits the Workplace

KATHY KENNEY-MARSHALL

I work with a bunch of losers. If that sounds harsh, don't stop reading. I have not turned into a brutally harsh judgmental type of person. These folks hold their banner in hope and they hold it high. They have labeled themselves and formed a club to which I am not invited. And they just might make me, a non-member based on stature, miserable by the time Valentine's Day rolls around.

The teachers and faculty in my building have decided that the New Year brings with it opportunities to unify and attempt to defeat the Battle of the Bulge. Whether it is three pounds or 30, those who want or need to lose weight have united in an attempt to become the "Biggest Loser". This contest is based on one of the newest Reality TV shows that bombard us nightly in newer, more questionable, and morally repugnant ways; Not pretty enough? There's *The Swan.* Not married and want to be? There's *The Bachelor* or *The Bachelorette.* Dying to be tossed into an unknown place to try to find your way home with no money attached to someone you can't stand? There's *The Race.* Tired of your wife? How about *Trading Spouses?* The list goes on and on, and while I do admit I am nearly fanatical about *Survivor* (the ONLY redeeming reality show in my humble opinion), I have long ago shed the desire to watch shows where desperate people go on National television to remake their bodies and their lives. Having said that, I am aware of the saying, Misery Loves Company, so the thought of 28 of my colleagues dieting together is neither offensive nor repugnant. They have created a way by which they will help each other lose unhealthy or unwanted weight through a respectful system of support, laughter, and maybe even a little constructive criticism. Nearly 40 percent of the faculty joined the Losers Club for a mere $20. This entry fee sweetens the pot (no pun intended) in the fight to shed unwanted calories and clothing sizes that have clung relentlessly on some, suddenly on others. Let's see, that's 28 people who stand to make $560 to lose the largest percent of their body weight. (Hmm ... maybe I should join ... I only weigh ... never mind.) I won't use their real names (because I would be forever entrenched in my already low "C" list social status ... though perhaps this column might raise me to "B" list person), but I will try to hide their identities by changing their names to protect the ... guilty? The 'loser wanna-be' applicants with whom I eat lunch however, just might ruin the next six weeks for non-members like me.

Today for example, I walked into a frigid 58 degree teacher's lounge to enjoy my turkey sandwich on whole wheat with mustard, my usual boring yet healthy lunch. With many of the other non-loser members' complaints about being cold, I took the liberty of turning up the heat. The 'losers' were walking the halls because the snow outside prevented the outside walk that was part of their diet plan. Upon entering the lunch room, the conversation turned quickly into a heated verbal assault on the sauna that the room had become in their absence. One member, "Bargie"* flushed and panting, complained that she couldn't eat in this heat. Another loser, "Beryl"*, joined in the whining over the raging temperature of 68 degrees. Entering the melee was "Bisa"*, sweating under her layers of a t-shirt, turtleneck, and sweater. While they were placated into eating their 3-point yogurts or fruit cups by my turning down the temperature to 65 degrees, they turned their attention to "Bim's"* lettuce choice for his loser club version of salad. "I would never eat *THAT* kind of lettuce." "God, no! It's only plain iceberg for me." "What kind of dressing *IS* that??" Poor "Bim", not only had he chosen to actually eat during lunchtime instead of exercising, he chose the wrong lettuce. And it was still too hot ... down another few degrees. I was beginning to turn blue.

> *Having said that, I am aware of the saying, Misery Loves Company, so the thought of 28 of my colleagues dieting together is neither offensive nor repugnant.*

But perhaps this is only the beginning of dieting grumpiness that will pass ... I hope. I myself was afraid to pull dessert out of my lunch bag for fear of reprisal even though it was merely a small container of pineapples in pear juice. And then there's the interesting juxtaposition of the "Loser Club" rules laying alongside the Girl Scout Cookie sign up sheet, the fudge, the chocolate cake, and the other `sugary sundries that are the normal lunch table embellishments. Hmm, this is going to be fascinating ... or deadly.

Reality Television Hits the Workplace

So I left the teacher's lounge, frostbitten , nervous, and yet hopeful for my colleagues that the initial difficulties of their challenge will begin to change into victorious good spirits as they move toward their goal of becoming the school's Biggest Loser. The intention (however contentious things become), is a great one; to help each other get to a healthy weight. In the words of my good friend and colleague, "Beryl", "even if you aren't the winner, you definitely will be a loser." And to become this kind of loser is a commendable title to share.

*These names have been altered to make them unrecognizable even to their closest friends, colleagues, and relatives. ◉

Older and Wiser
KATHY KENNEY-MARSHALL

Birthdays are a funny thing. When you're six or seven, this day is as excitedly anticipated as Christmas. You look forward to getting older and enjoying the perceived benefits that go with your newfound "older-ness". I remember how I couldn't wait to be 10. No more baby single digit birthdays, and being the youngest, that was huge. But sadly, being 10 turned out to be a whole lot like being nine.

Then I couldn't wait to be 13 because, well, all kinds of wonderful things happen when you're 13. Wonderful my foot, I got my period. For some girls, this is a rite of passage, the beginning of being a woman. I found it a disgusting waste of time spent in the bathroom and a limitation of activities for five to seven days each month. Some birthday present.

Once I resigned myself to that "gift" of becoming older, I set my sights on the next great age; 16. Sweet 16, when I would finally be allowed to go on real car dates and I could finally get my driver's license. The dating part was ok, though I don't recall being "over-booked" with the boys. And I never did get my license that year because, again, as the youngest, my parents had learned from my older siblings that kids ruin cars. So if they were not going to let me use their car, in parent logic, why bother with a license.

But the magical age of 18 was right around the corner. Back then, 18 was the age you could go to clubs and drink legally. Of course, that was the year the drinking age changed to 21. I could vote, and I did, but that coveted legal beer was three more years in the waiting. Somehow, I was beginning to suspect that birthday magic lost instead of gained its appeal as I grew older. But 18 wasn't all bad. I went away to college and finally, through the tutelage of my college roomie, got my driver's license.

21, was going to be the magic number I was sure. And it was pretty good if my aging memory isn't deceiving me. I graduated college and got married just three weeks later. Not a bad birthday gift that year. I found myself with my new husband thumbing our way through Ireland enjoying the greenery and the generosity of the Irish. It was a wonderful time. I was beginning to believe in birthdays again.

Time tends to fly once you have children. I also received another birthday gift that year, albeit belated ... when my first child was born just nine months and two weeks after my wedding day. A perfect gift wrapped in pink. Twenty months later came another bundle of joy, this one more Christmas than birthday gift and the final best birthday gift arrived just five days before I turned 30.

As I approach this birthday many people ask me, "So what? Are you 29 again? Hahaha!" I wouldn't want to be 29 again if you paid me. I was nine-plus months pregnant with a watermelon sized kid, could barely walk, and hadn't slept because the creature inside decided to take up kickboxing in his fifth month. But I remember leaving the twenty-ninth year. Since I was 30, I was certain that my husband had planned a grand party for me. But no party, no guests, no hoopla at all. He actually thought I might be a little tired from giving birth to a nine-and-a-half-pound baby, inconsiderate cad. He frantically made phone calls to friends, family, and a few neighbors I didn't know who came for cake and ice cream.

As I pass into the early to mid 40s*, I think I actually like where I am and don't wish to go back to any one age that was better than now. I have kids who are growing up and flourishing. I have a marriage that is 21 years strong and still going. And most of all, there are no major illnesses or tragedies that I have to deal with. Life is pretty good.

So what I've decided is that a birthday is just that, a day. Perhaps a day that we think about what we've done with ourselves in the past 365 days, but if I just live well and accept what life gives me every day, I know I find gifts that mean much more than the ones my family and friends wrap up this one day a year just for me.

Please don't misinterpret that statement, I will be expecting the usual pile of presents this evening, along with my chocolate cake.

*I've recently turned 50 so it's been a few years since the writing of this column. Life gets better and better! ◉

Slice of Heaven and a $20,000 Lunch

KATHY KENNEY-MARSHALL

I'm not the type of person who does things on the spur of the moment. It's not that I'm not flexible, but when it comes to my social life, i am the kind of person who has to plan to be spontaneous.

So when my mother talked about taking me to Martha's Vineyard for a few days on short notice, I surprised even myself when I threw caution to the wind and said yes.

"Pack light!" was my mother's advice. "Nobody dresses up on the Island. Just bring your Vineyard casuals." 'Sure,' I thought, 'whatever that means.' I managed to cram enough of what I imagined to be 'Vineyard casuals' into a rolling suitcase and a carry on canvas bag.

We were to be staying at The Harborside Inn in Edgartown in a room whose balcony overlooked the courtyard where there was to be an auction the afternoon we arrived. As it turns out, this was a biggie. It was called the Possible Dreams Auction and the money that was made that day would go to benefit Martha's Vineyard Community Servies.

Hmmmm ... an island as affluent as this needed community services? Who knew? Author Art Buchwald hosted and was actually one of the auctioneers. I was a little star struck as I saw Mike Wallace sitting not more than 20 yards from the balcony where I stood watching.

The prosperous people of Martha's Vineyard were bidding high on the likes of paintings done by local artist Jules Feiffer, a walk-on role for Larry David's Curb Your Enthusiasm television show, and tickets to Super Bowl XXXIX to name a few.

I was in awe of how much money these people had to play with. For example, for a mere $5,000, a lucky family that consisted of two adults and up to three children between the ages of 7 to14 were to spend the day with Tom Hamilton, the bassist for the group Aerosmith. He and his wife, along with their two kids would take them to their home for a day of tennis, swimming and a barbeque.

Another couple shelled out $21,000 to have lunch with Mike Wallace and his wife. I wondered how Mike felt when Walter Cronkite's lunch sold for $25,000. I'm sure he was just a little miffed.

But my favorite winning bid came from a boy of not more that 13 or 14. His bid? $38,000 for a private sunset concert for him and 19 of his closest friends at the waterfront home of Livingston Taylor. At 14, I was lucky to have $38 and for sure, if I was going to shell that kind of dough out for a sunset concert I'm pretty sure I would have preferred Aerosmith, (since one of them was there), or Queen. I love Livingston Taylor, but a teenager? Oh how times have changed!

What I really noticed though was that even though I didn't bid on anything that day, there were lots of others who didn't either. And all of us regular folks, the non-bidders like me, got to be one of the "beautiful people" that day for just a little while.

At one point in the afternoon when Livingston Taylor got up to sing, I closed my eyes as his crisp soothing voice sang, God Bless America, a song that can dampen my eyes any time. All the people, the rich, the not so rich, the volunteers, and the service people who keep the Inn clean, in those few moments, all became one. It started slowly, but soon everyone sang softly along with clarity and unity for the simple beauty of a song about America.

With only the accompaniment of ocean sounds, it was probably the most precious thing at the auction that day and it didn't cost a thing. When we all finished the applause was thunderous and joyful. For me, the auction ended there on a high note with something priceless and awe inspiring.

My mother and I spent two more days on the island riding around in a rented red convertible. I must admit, we looked pretty good in it too! We saw most of this charming little piece of heaven where the rich build enormous houses with exquisite views of the ocean. We walked into the finest restaurants and galleries. We perused jewelry far out of our price range and luxuriated in the attention of the flawlessly dressed sales clerks.

We stopped at many little shops where plastic and canvas flip-flops sold for $50 and if, God forbid, you wanted those little brown leather sandals with the little bells, you had to shell out $495!

Needless to say, I came home with some fudge for my kids and some discounted Black Dog t-shirts. And although I still haven't figured out what 'Vineyard Casual' means, I suspect it means anything you pay too much for even though it looks like you could have bought it at Old Navy!

It was such a fun three days playing among the rich and famous and yet, I was happy to come home to my family, who I think are truly the "Beautiful People." ◉

Super-sizing: Boon or Bust?
KATHY KENNEY-MARSHALL

Everyone is super-sizing these days – from the fad in denim where if your boxers aren't showing the pants are too tight, to laundry detergent bottles so big it's a Herculean endeavor to do the wash. The argument at my house often revolves around fast food. My sons want everything super-sized; from French fries to soft drinks that when super-sized could quench the thirst of a small village in Ethiopia – or at least a large family of 10.

Bigger is better, or so the saying goes in the advertising world anyway. I'm just not so sure I agree, unless we're talking about my checking account which is never big enough!

It came up again a few years ago in a more important life altering way from my own sister. She was a 43-year-old single mom who decided that it was time to super-size a part of her body. I'll not say what part, I'll only give you a hint; she didn't enroll in a graduate program to increase her brain size, but began frequenting Victoria's Secret. You understand.

I couldn't believe it, perhaps because I have undergone numerous surgeries that were not elective, I couldn't understand how anyone would let someone cut into their body voluntarily! But apparently her AA size was not acceptable, and perhaps she thought that this was at least partly to blame for her single status. So off she went for her personal upgrade.

I received an email from her shortly after the surgery. "UGH!" I assumed that the "ugh" was referring to the excruciating pain she was experiencing from having some kind of water filled balloon shoved into her chest through incisions no larger than my thumb-nail. I was right. After just a few days however, she felt well enough to have her 19-year-old daughter drive the hour long ride to my house to show off her new additions.

My husband was nervous. "Do I look at them? Am I supposed to hug her when I say hello? Is a compliment required or even appropriate?" All reasonable questions to which I had no immediate answers. This would be new to all of us. "Just shake her hand and maintain eye contact," was my final word of advice as they pulled into the driveway.

After a quick greeting, it was off to the bathroom for all the girls; my daughter, my niece, and me to see the new Cs! After a painful looking hike of a now too small sweatshirt, followed by a too small t-shirt, and finally a VERY tight sports bra, we saw them.

Hmmm ... what does one say when the proudly displayed skin is crusted, bruised, and markedly swollen? I decided that I would use the line my husband saves for when I get a haircut he doesn't like; "Well, how do you like them?"

After the 'show,' I gave the matter a lot of thought and decided that while I would never opt for this type of "enhancement," there might be some advantages that most of us don't think of. For example, if my sister ever spills her coffee, she won't be in danger of scalding her lap, her nether-regions, or worse staining her favorite white pants! It won't hurt up there because all of her skin nerve sensation is gone, at least for now. Another advantage would make bath time a rather enjoyable experience. Since they are so new and so high, she can rest a glass of Chardonnay and a book very comfortably up there and never worry about wet pages! During meals, her lap will remain shielded from dinner spills and if standing in the rain, her shoes will always stay dry. True, she'll never be able to sleep on her stomach again and she will have to shell out a small fortune in new lingerie and sweaters, but when she drops a French fry from her super-size box next time she goes to McDonald's, she can simply look down and pick it up with her teeth.

A tempting thought, but I've always hated McDonalds. ◉

Surgery: No Laughing Matter
KATHY KENNEY-MARSHALL

I've been wondering about whether to write this column. It's an embarrassing matter but I decided that I would write it when I almost ripped out my newly acquired titanium staples while sharing this story with a good friend, (Lynne, it's ok to talk about it now).

I had surgery recently and it's not a pleasant kind to discuss, like say, a root canal or a vascectomy. I can't really bring myself to tell exactly what was ailing me, but suffice to say that parts of my body that should stay inside of me, were trying to get out. Great! Not only do I have ground my kids, I have to ground my internal organs. (Liver, Kidneys, Bladder, you must stay in place until ... well ... until I die!)

Surgery is no laughing matter, but it can have its humorous moments. As I lay in the pre-op area waiting for the anesthesiologist to inject a relaxing agent into my IV line, my husband tried to calm my jitters by reading to me from Uncle John's Bathroom Reader; a book full of totally useless but interesting information. I found out, for example, that I weigh less than one African Elephants ear. I'm not sure if I will ever need this fact, but if perhaps I make it onto Jeopardy someday, I will be the first contestant to ring my buzzer if the answer is: "Approximate weight of an African Elephants Ear". BUZZ! "Yes, Kathy" "Alex, the question is, "What weighs more than me!" RIGHT!

The greatest thing about surgery, I suppose, is the fact that there are doctors out there who know the human anatomy (if not the weight of an elephant's ear) so well, that they can go in there and slide things back into place or remove things that don't belong with the ease of say, making a batch of brownies.

Directions:
- Reduce temperature in Operating Room to induce frostbite into patient.
- Toss semi-frozen patient onto even colder metal slab and twist patient into positions not possible when awake.

- Shove garden hose size breathing tube down patient's throat taking care not to bruise the uvula or surrounding area.
- Use WWII torture instrument to widen small orifices to unnatural sizes and leave in long enough to cause excruciating pain that awakens patient.
- Administer more medication to stop the distracting screaming from half frozen patient.
- Use sharpened instrument to move or remove pieces of patient that may not belong ... or that just look ugly.
- Staple patient back together.
- Wake, medicate and send patient home.

It's easy. Right?

Having gone through this process recently, I can attest to this Betty Crocker style of surgery. It's quick, easy, and before you know it, the surgeons are onto their next box of brownies ... ah, their next patient. Then the nurses in the post-op area kindly ask you to rate your pain on a scale of one to ten; ten being the worst. They were a little confused when I could barely whisper 12. "12? There is no 12 dear. They didn't teach us 12 in nursing school." She missed my point. I needed narcotics and I needed them fast. The unfortunate part of this was that I could not reach up, grab her by the kitten covered jacket and scream "If I don't get pain medication quickly, I will kill every kitten on your jacket." Kitten killing is not something I would ordinarily condone, but the feeling of having been beaten, cut, and mishandled from the inside out, outweighed my allegiance to a kitten's right to live, even if it was a cartoon kitten on a jacket.

Finally, medication flowing, I fell into a chemically induced state of near-relaxation. When the pain level was tolerable, I was brought home to my own bed to sleep off the narcotics that would have killed a small rhino.

Now, feeling much better, I am able to look at this experience and be truly thankful for the doctors and nurses who put me back together. As with every trial and tribulation in my life, I try to pull the positive out of my experiences. What I learned from this past surgery is that I am lucky to have doctors and nurses who know what they are doing. Second, I am fortunate that my family and friends care for me and are there when I need them. I also learned that the human body is an intricate machine that has more that goes right than goes wrong. But more interesting, I learned that an African Elephants ear weighs more than I do ... fascinating. I'm eager for the folks from Jeopardy have try-outs in the Boston Area ... I'm a shoo-in. ◉

Tax Amnesty: Was it Worth the Headache?

KATHY KENNEY-MARSHALL

At 7:07 that Saturday morning, my husband, Paul, and I entered the Best Buy store in Braintree to take advantage of the first tax amnesty day ever offered in Massachusetts. Since becoming more interested in writing, we decided it was time to get a new computer that would be solely for my writing endeavors; in other words a "kid-free" zone.

Paul, being the every-bolstering spouse, offered his advice: "If you want to be a writer, you have to have the tools of a writer." Nice, wonderful, so supportive! Turns out, there was an ulterior motive ... he wanted a plasma TV! What the heck, off we went in search of our toys.

We were smart. We went out on Friday evening to comparison shop and had our purchases chosen ahead of time. Being seasoned day-after-Thanksgiving shoppers, we knew the horrors of the indecisive consumer. We wanted to be prepared.

It was busy in the computer section of the store, but being prepared paid off as we spied the young man who had helped us the night before and, as promised, he had our computer all ready for us to take away. All we had to do now was stand in the oppressively long checkout line at the "Geek Squad" counter where a "Geek" would scare us into spending more money on service plans. (Lest anyone become offended by my use of the word geek, it is not my term of endearment or one of insult. It is an actual title that is used by the company as is "sales associate" or "manager.")

If we refused said service plans, worms, Trojans, and other unmentionable creatures would enter our new computer rendering it lifeless. And in fine print, we learned that we would lose our second and third born child if that were to occur – a tempting thought, but we bought them anyway.

If all that wasn't enough to make the morning glorious in our savings of the dreaded sales tax, the topper of all came next; REBATES! Rebates sound so terrific on paper. A whole different "geek" handed us a mound of forms we'd need to fill out and send in to the Rebate Gods somewhere. It's easy and self-explanatory "rebate Geek" promised us. He was a smooth talker and a fast talker too. Seinfeld fans know what I mean – and we believed him. That is ... until we got home.

The forms looked easy at first; you know, name address, phone number, etc. Then came the rules. For rebate #1, I needed to write down the model number and the serial number. The model number was easy as it was right on the box. Now the serial number shouldn't be too hard, I expected, until I couldn't see the actual words 'serial number' anywhere on the box or the receipt. Hmmm ... was it the huge line of numbers and letters that followed the initials, S/N? Yes, that seemed right; cnc87jyoce8u86iokehkIt9999. Ok, all set. Until the other lower case 'sn' appeared on another side of the box: qpz09ikmneo. Right ... unless the serial CODE, pgy99023651hn87 that was printed under the box was what they were looking for.

Rebates sound so terrific on paper. A whole different "geek" handed us a mound of forms we'd need to fill out and send in to the Rebate Gods somewhere.

A conundrum unfolded before my eyes. I opened the box and there, on the side of the computer tower, under the Styrofoam, the packing paper, and the corrugated cardboard that took three of us to rip off, were the words, "serial number." Thank God!

The next item on the master list of instructions: Please include the actual or a photocopy of the proof of purchase including the UPC code. This I can do, I thought optimistically. It only took a box cutter, a pair of scissors, a serrated knife, and four Advil tablets for the headache that was emerging to remove the UPC stickers from the three boxes. But apparently copies of these bulky pieces of coardboard are not acceptable in all situations. I looked at the three rebate forms. All three stated that copies or originals could be sent. This was good news since I needed these copies for two of the three forms.

When one more question came up on these "easy" forms, I called the 800 number. After waiting through 29 minutes of prere-corded commercials and the stilted voices of operators telling me how very much they appreciated my call, I discovered that copies were not accepted for all rebates. At this point, I was ready to forget about the

Tax Amnesty: Was it Worth the Headache?

$300 worth of rebates. But somehow, I forged on and completed, hopefully correctly, all three forms. I hope I put the right originals in the right envelopes with the right serial numbers and code numbers, etc. I figured I owed it to Paul who had decided against the plasma TV since there are not such products under the $2,500 limit to qualify for the tax amnesty. He'll have to wait for the prices to come down. Smart move since as with all new technology, the prices will certainly lower to more reasonable ones in the not too distant future.

In reflecting on our experience with the lines, the Geeks, the purchase process in general, and especially the rebate process, we've come up with a way to avoid the lure of tax-free-earlier-than-is-humane-shopping-days that might tempt us in the future. We're going to shop in New Hampshire ☉!

The Magic of Hometown Baseball
KATHY KENNEY-MARSHALL

The baseball season has begun. Not only was it Opening Day at Fenway Park, it was Opening Day for the high school where my son is finishing his senior year. After enjoying a day sporting temperatures in the 70s over the weekend, today's first home game found me donning my winter coat, gloves, hat, scarf, and of course a heavy turtleneck sweater. The sun was shining, but apparently nobody told the weatherman that it was April.

That's how it is here in New England, Bermuda shorts to Shetland sweaters.

I was prepared.

As I sat in the bleachers, (hard cold wood that leaves me wondering who designed these God-forsaken slabs we call seats) changing positions to follow the setting sun, I reveled in what I have come to think of as early season baseball culture. Though the layers of baseball fan wear change as the season progresses, there is one thing I can count on, though I never think of it from September until April: baseball speak.

People just sound different during a baseball game. Normal folks who carry on perfectly normal conversations in every other place on earth, adopt a lilt of baseball rhetoric that is as American as apple pie. As I sat today, huddled in my faux fur lined, but appropriately spring colored down parka, I listened and was lulled into a state of almost perfect relaxation.

"There ya go Matt, boy ... atta way!"
"Good-eye Rob, thatta way kid!"
"Two down, make'm work Bobby!"
"You got'm kid, swing at it!"
"SWING Batta ... that's two!"

I realized that one of the things I love most about this game, especially kids' baseball, is the language. The tone. The emotion that accompanies each phrase, each shout out to a teammate. It's almost musical and each player, each parent, each fan, understands the words that no one would use outside of the baseball field:

"Hum it in there, baby"
"Blow it by'm"
"Can-o-corn kid"
"Give'm a hook, man"
"1 more, atta way, make him work it"

Though it's more fun to win, even losses feel like home when you're on the field watching the kids play.

It makes me wonder about the million dollar players that we pay so much of our regular-people-money to see. Do they love the game, live the game, breathe and feel the game like these boys? I wonder if they are yelling to each other out there, the words of encouragement that our high school, middle school, even our little leaguers are chanting, feeling the ball as it hits their gloves, or the breeze as it just misses. Do they feel the real joy of catching a fly ball, or are they thinking about the bonus that will surely come after that magic number home run?

> *People just sound different during a baseball game. Normal folks who carry on perfectly normal conversations in every other place on earth, adopt a lilt of baseball rhetoric that is as American as apple pie.*

These boys that play hometown ball are the lucky ones, I think. They have the innocent dream of being in the big leagues. With every, "Atta-way kid", they picture themselves in the uniform of stars, not realizing that this time in their lives is the time that character is made. But what do I know? I'm only a mom, sitting on the sidelines in April in a winter coat, cherishing every strike, every ball, every hit. I wear my sideline uniform and love every moment, every steal, every run, and even every miss because I know that this is what dreams are made of. This is a part of my boys' forever, the part of their lives that we will all look back on, wherever their lives take them, and smile. A time when they can scream with enthusiasm and complete honesty; "Guy likes the heat! Live in the junkyard!" and know that it means to give it all you got.

That's what baseball is, after all. A time to have fun, play fair, love the game, and give it all you've got. ☉

The Morning After

KATHY KENNEY-MARSHALL

Not too many people know this about me, but I am an addict. I am not ashamed to admit it any longer because my addiction causes no harm to anyone or anything except my own thighs. I am addicted to chocolate. There, I've said it. I'm out. But I don't crave the fancy kinds, like Godiva, Lindt, Toberlone, or any of the varieties with names I can't pronounce. I leave those to the chocolate snobs. My addiction? Plain M&Ms. Don't buy me the peanut, almond, or crunchy, I'm a chocolate purist. I love the smell, the taste, and the way they seemingly crunch and melt all at the same time. I love the sound as I pour a new bag into my bubble-gum type of dispenser. But it doesn't stop there. My third grade classroom is a veritable shrine to this confection. I adore all of the trinkets and paraphernalia that goes along with it. I thank God every day for the marketing moguls all around the world, or at least in Las Vegas and Jersey. I have the plastic M&M vending machines of every variety. I have M&M containers for my paper clips, rubber bands, and thumb tacks. M&M coffee mugs of every shape and color hold color coordinated pens, pencils, and markers. I have an M&M tape dispenser, notepad holder, and even my boring tan classroom telephone has been replaced with a talking red M&M who calls, "Hey, come and get this! It's probably for you!" There is not a corner in my classroom that does not sport some form of M&M "art." And yes, I really do eat them every day. Once in a while I share, but for the most part, when it comes to the kids and the candy, I have a hands-off policy. The children love the décor, but are not allowed to touch. They learn quickly; I am very easy to get along with, as long as they don't touch my stuff. Like I said, not many people know this about me (uh-huh), but I am afraid I am a fanatic.

However, having said all that, I feel as strongly about my next statement as I do about M&Ms: I really hate Halloween. I suppose that's not entirely truthful. It's the day AFTER Halloween that I despise. Especially this year because Halloween falls on a Sunday; a weekend day, yet a school night. As if Mondays are not hard enough, this year on Sunday night, all elementary school teachers will fill with a dread something akin to a morning with no caffeine and a classroom of one hundred eight-year-olds instead of the usual 24. This year, instead of dragging themselves up the stairs in an 'oh-my-God-is-the-weekend-over-type-stupor' as is the norm for a Monday morning, the kids will charge up the stairs screaming excitedly over the proceeds of their trick-or-treating escapades of the night. They'll compare, brag, and embellish their profits as if weekend fly-fishing enthusiasts. Ask any teacher and they'll agree, it's a morning of misery. The children will flood in like salmon swimming upstream, trying to cram themselves, all 24 at the same time, through the classroom door. They will topple over one another to reach their desks overturning chairs in their attempt to sit down. But their sugar saturated bodies might miss and at least four or five will end up on the floor being stepped on by another pinball (bing-bing) pupil. The customary Monday morning assignment in my room, Weekend News, will be hastily scribbled while many line up at the electric pencil sharpener and attempt to sharpen another broken pencil. On this once-a-year,(have I said Thank God yet?), sugar high, a pencil is certain to be forgotten and a finger may be attempted to be sharpened instead. Any veteran teacher knows this and comes prepared bearing an extra large dark French-Roast from Starbucks with two extra shots of espresso. The experienced teacher stands a chance against the chaos that is spelled H-A-L-L-O-W-E-E-N. She wears her combat gear; sturdy khakis, sensible shoes, and a referee whistle. She looks equipped, ready to act, and unafraid, for the candy- encumbered child smells fear like a rabid dog. Yes, it takes an alert mind and nerves of steel to man a Monday Morning Sugar Hangover. I'm sure I can do it.

But first, I think I'll need a few M&Ms. ◉

> *My addiction? Plain M&Ms. Don't buy me the peanut, almond, or crunchy, I'm a chocolate purist. I love the smell, the taste, and the way they seemingly crunch and melt all at the same time.*

Choosing to See Surprises
KATHY KENNEY-MARSHALL

Do you ever find surprises in ordinary things? Occasionally I find myself being caught off guard. At times when I least suspect it, I round the same corners I travel every day and see the same things, yet they strike me as extraordinarily different. Perhaps there really is a difference, or maybe I allow myself to see them differently for a moment. I'm not sure, but either way, it has a way of changing the way I approach my day. Autumn especially has a way of giving us all these delightful opportunities to take a glimpse into ourselves.

While driving on Rt. 128 at 6:45 one morning, the sun was casting its light on the trees in a particular way that made the sides of the highway burst with beauty. I actually found myself thankful that the traffic was crawling at 10 miles per hour because I had the luxury of looking at the array of orange, crimson, and gold, loving the way the damp leaves seems to sparkle like jewels. Then to add to the landscape, hundreds of starlings flew out of the trees in a formation that nearly stopped traffic altogether. They swooped down over the cars as if the hundreds of us were part of nature.

As they disappeared into another group of trees, this group, not as densely populated with color, I was struck by the thought that although we love the colors of fall, it is the beginning of death for the leaves. If only we could look at human death in that same way. Certainly I am not speaking about the tragedy of young lives lost, but for those who suffer long periods of time and for those who have aged into the dusk of their lives with the richness of the color of leaves in fall, the best we can say is that it is a blessing and hopefully we can accept it as one of life's natural processes. This doesn't make us any less sad at our loss, but we understand the life's circle that does indeed have an end here on earth unlike those leaves that are reborn each spring.

As autumn's colors fade to brown and leave the trees naked to withstand the coming winter, many of us go through a different sense of loss. There is a condition called Seasonal Affective Disorder where many people suffer from depressive symptoms as the days get shorter and we find ourselves in the dark. The nights seem too long and the days too short. I often feel as I drive to work on that same stretch of 128 where the beauty of the trees took my breath away in autumn, the starkness of those same trees and how cold they make me feel. Then the first snow covers them lightly, changing the landscape to one that sparkles with bright newness and hope, and I find myself surprised at their beauty once again.

At times like these I begin to wonder why I let the simple pleasures take my breath away only once in a while. One of my favorite poets wrote about looking at ordinary things differently. In her poem, Valentine for Ernest Mann, Naomi Shihab Nye wrote about a man who gave his wife two skunks as a valentine.

"He couldn't understand why she was crying.
He thought they had such beautiful eyes.
Nothing was ugly just because the world said so.
So he took those skunks and reinvented them as valentines and they became beautiful.
At least to him."

As we travel through this time of year; the time when we watch color fade with the time of daylight hours, and the time we should be thankful for what blessings we have, I want to think of Ernest Mann. When we leave for work and get home in the darkness, I want to be thankful for a full moon in a clear night sky. I want to be able to appreciate the colors of dying leaves and the beauty of new snow. And more than that, I want to be mindful of the love of family and the warmth of home. Though surprises around the corner may lift one's spirits, maybe we can all choose to surprise ourselves more regularly. It's worth a try and it might just make those dark nights more comforting than just too darn long.

The Evils of the Remote Control
KATHY KENNEY-MARSHALL

There are arguments occurring in family living rooms everywhere. Mostly women, whether it be the small or grown-up variety have been waging a battle with men over a little device called the remote control. While some savvy families have actually read the manuals and learned how to control everything in their homes, from the television to the toilet with just one remote, more of us have seven or eight kicking around. Worse than that, most of us haven't a clue as to how they work. I have spent many an evening waiting for someone, my husband, my son, the neighbor's four year old to come home and turn on the evening news for me. Some would say it's a very little problem to have but I know different. I'm considering a letter to my local congressman to ban the use of the remote control, not because I can't figure out how to use it, and certainly not because if a male is watching at my house, the channel is annoyingly changed every 10.5 seconds, but because I am concerned about a bigger problem ... our nation's health.

Obesity is a skyrocketing problem here in America. While sitting home on a rainy Saturday night recently, I figured out why. I also realized why there was a population explosion immediately before that period of time when obesity became as prevalent. The culprit in both cases is the television remote.

I remember when I was a child, we actually had to get up to turn the station, which is why parents had many children. They needed someone to change the channel for them. Thankfully, there weren't too many to choose from back then. But I suspect that there is another condition that may have peaked in incidence around the time when we were introduced to hundreds of millions of channels but before the widespread popularity of the remote control that in our house has been nicknamed "the magic box". That condition of course would be carpal tunnel syndrome.

You may be thinking by now, "she's lost it". Obesity, a population explosion, and carpal tunnel syndrome are the fault of the remote control/magic box? While you are probably correct, let me explain my thinking.

If your house is anything at all like mine, there is not a commercial we've ever seen with the exception of the Superbowl when we must see the ads for which companies are willing to pay millions of dollars per second. When there is a commercial break in my house, my husband/son/daughter/uninvited guest must find something else to watch for 60 seconds – two minutes. Even a few minutes of Mr. Rogers reruns are more tempting than commercials that sing the praises of cheese. If there is a jingle or a product being peddled, it's not watched.

I, on the other hand, grew up looking for commercials. I wanted to "be a Pepper", even though I hated Dr. Pepper. I didn't mind scraping my knees because, "I was stuck on Band-aids and Band-aids stuck on me." I loved that "finger-lickin' good Kentucky Fried" and "I deserved a break today" (though you couldn't get me to go to McDonald's in disguise today, I still sing the jingle.) My boloney had a first name, and my stomach ache medication was the "last name in relief". I was a commercial junkie.

So where am I going with all this? Fast forward to today but with no "magic box". There are 4,578 channels to choose from not including On Demand. IF you were to change the channel during every commercial break, there would be no obesity because you'd actually have to get yourself off the couch to change channels. Then you'd develop carpal tunnel syndrome from turning the circular knob on the television around the 4,578 choices, (and probably miss half of the 6 hour long epic movie you were watching to begin with). As for the population explosion, well, most folks with those fancy wall size plasma televisions (without remotes remember), might be short-sighted enough to have just one child who would change the channel for them. However, the smarter pairs would have two or three extras for the certain time when the first born came down with a bad case of carpal tunnel syndrome. Then the second, then the third, and so on. The more children you have, the more television viewing pleasure you would have. We'd surely keep our country's hand surgeons busy and would solve our channel changing problem.

Then again ... we're right back to that obesity problem for those parents. But there just might be a commercial that will tell us how to handle that.

"Honey, where's the youngest channel changer ... I mean, where's Michael?" ☉

There's a Law For *THAT*?

KATHY KENNEY-MARSHALL

When I was in high school, we planted a time capsule. In it were items that my class imagined would give future generations a peek into what things were like "in the olden days." My memory isn't great, but I do remember a few things we chose to include; an eight track cassette tape, Freshen Up gum, a pair of Earth Shoes, and perhaps something that had been tie-dyed. The same thing was going on all over the country with high school seniors burying their present so that the future would get a look at the past.

What might have been more interesting however, would be the rules that were voted into law. I'm not sure what laws were enacted in the 1970's, but I took the liberty to look into some from all over the United States. For example, I am relieved not to be living in Michigan because there, my hair would legally belong to my husband and therefore I would need his written permission to cut it. In Maine, it is illegal to step off plane in flight while in Canada, (yes, I know it's not in our country, but they're neighbors and it fit this column), you may not board a plane in flight. It's illegal to mispronounce Arkansas in Arkansas, you may not swim on dry land in California, and in Alaska, kangaroos are not allowed in barber shops at any time.

If you do your homework, (and by the way, May 6 is National No Homework Day, so don't do it then), you can find many strange laws right here in the Commonwealth. You may have even broken one or two. For example, it is unlawful for a Massachusetts mourner to eat more than three sandwiches after a funeral. In Holyoke, it is against the law to water your lawn when it is raining. You might have broken this law if you shower in the morning because in Massachusetts, it is illegal to go to bed without a full bath. This one may be particularly confusing for Bostonians for there are several laws regarding the practice of bathing; No more than two baths may be taken within the city limits at one time, no baths may be taken on Sunday, and you may not take a bath at any time without a prescription!

Naturally, many of these laws were made during different periods of time in our history, which makes me quite happy that none of my three children made time capsules containing some of the more ridiculous laws that have been enacted in their childhoods; the most recent one about bullying is one that would and should cause embarrassment to all of us as a culture.

> *You might have broken this law if you shower in the morning because in Massachusetts, it is illegal to go to bed without a full bath.*

While discussing this at lunch the other day, a colleague brought this law up as a concern we should all have. I agreed when he said, "Shouldn't it just be common sense that bullying shouldn't be condoned? Why did we need a law telling us this?" Well, in response, I could have pointed out that we had to have a law to make people wash their hands after going to the bathroom, a reality that children learn as soon as they are potty trained. Why should our lawmakers have to write common sense into law?

Yes, it is a tremendous loss for the family of the teen in South Hadley who took her own life because it became too much for her to bear. I won't debate the devastating effects of being the target of bullies. However, this is an issue that does not belong in the Halls of Justice or our Legislative Sessions. Neither does the act of washing one's hands. But apparently we, as a country, have lost the ability to know the difference between right and wrong. Today, for example, I saw a grown woman of about 50 dip her hands into the desert bar at Whole Foods, lick her fingers, then scoop out a little more. I may have to call my Legislator tomorrow morning. ☉

Ignorance is Sometimes Bliss
KATHY KENNEY-MARSHALL

You're never too old to learn something new though sometimes I'd rather remain ignorant.

Take the other day while waiting at the orthodontist's office with my son; I picked up the most intellectual piece of reading material on the table, (People magazine), and read an article about a couple from the Midwest who were having a little difficulty with the local constabulary. The newlyweds were shown holding their two month old daughter, "Grapefruit," (not her real name, but close enough), beaming as all new parents do. The story unfolded dramatically in front of me. The husband in the picture had just been released on bail. He had been arrested for having consensual sex with his wife. How could this be, I wondered? As I read on, I discovered that his wife was merely 14 years old, which would explain the feety-pajamas she was wearing, the pink bunny barrettes in her hair, and the braces that sported multicolored metal. It was then that I learned my new fact for the day. Turns out, in certain states, it's legal to get married when you are 14. But the most dramatic fact I learned through this mind stimulating magazine was that our very own state of Massachusetts is one of only two states in the country where it is legal for a youngster to get married at the ripe old age of 12 ... as long as she gets a note signed by her mommy.

I was horrified, mortified, and all sorts of 'fied'. I thought about my 13 year old son who was sitting beside me, waiting to see how long he would need to wear silver in his mouth and wondered what kind of a husband he would make at his age when he can't even remember to cut his toenails and the most coveted item for purchase these days is a package of baseball cards from e-Bay.

The couple in the magazine was able to get married in the only other state in the country that allows prepubescent marriage, Kansas. The couple's home state doesn't allow children to get married until they are 16 making this an unrecognized marriage. The husband, a 22 year old dishwasher who makes about $9/hour, fell in love with his wife when she was 12. When she got pregnant the following year, he proposed and the youngster's mother thought the idea of marriage was just fine, so she wrote her a note. They crossed the state line to Kansas, got married and moved home where state officials there call their marital relations, statutory rape, a crime that comes with stiff penalties and probable jail time.

This story got me thinking about milestone ages for growing adolescents and what these milestones will now mean for this 14-year-old mother. In Massachusetts, she would not be able to quit school until the age of 16, making those high school daycare centers handy. Also, the legal driving age is 16 ½ which means that by the time her baby is almost three, she will finally be able to bring little "Grapefruit", to her doctor's appointments herself because there are no car seats in school buses.

When she turns 17, she can be tried as an adult if she commits a crime, yet if she committed the same crime now, she would be tried as a juvenile. She'd better get any law breaking impulses out of her system within the next three years.

Of course when she turns 18, she can vote; a vital responsibility since she may need help if her marriage doesn't work out since over 50% of all children who get married will get divorced. Usually this is over something very important like whether to watch *Seinfeld* or *Simpsons* reruns. At 18, she can also sign up to fight for her country and join the armed forces which she will be fully prepared to do after years of mothering. Motherhood tends to toughen you up like that.

Then there is that milestone age that all teens wait anxiously for, 21, the age where you can drink legally. By then, little Grapefruit will be in the second grade and if there aren't a whole bunch of other little citrus fruits crawling around, she can hire a babysitter and go clubbing with her friends, assuming she still has friends because she's lost much of her childhood buddies to college or the work force and the dating scene.

As we left the orthodontist office, my son was unhappy with the sentence of two to three years in metal mouthpieces. I left unhappy too, for the dental bill I was facing for sure, but more for the lost childhood of a little girl I don't even know. But I also left feeling thankful for my son's messy room, mountains of laundry, and his boyhood lamentation for baseball cards. ◉

Leaving It to the Experts
KATHY KENNEY-MARSHALL

Whoever said; "Guests are like fish, after three days, they stink," couldn't have been more right. We'd been the hosts of houseguests for a few weeks, and now that they have departed, I can finally rest. At first we were polite letting them have the run of the house, more or less, shooing them out of our way when necessary. But when they became so comfortable they starting inviting their friends and relatives, we began to lose patience. And finally, when our favorite cereals were being consumed, when we had to throw away the Bisquick, when they started throwing breakfast socials on our kitchen counters – we did what any normal family would do; we tried to kill them.

I am, of course, talking about every picnickers pest; ants. At first, one or two seemed normal because my back door is broken and won't close properly. A few critters could crawl over the threshold on high adventure to the potential treats in my cluttered kitchen. But one afternoon as I began picking up "rinsed out" soda cans from the counter, I found my forearm engulfed with scattering six-legged black insects. I remained as calm as I could while screaming, brushing them off into the sink where I ran the water, and then let my Insinkerator do the rest. I was immediately filled with murderous guilt. I had probably just demolished a mother, father, several dozen offspring, and probably a few distant cousin ants. I wasn't cut out for this. I called the exterminator.

If my dad was still alive, I would have called him instead. He would have welcomed the challenge; after all, every Christmas since my children have understood spoken language, he offered to buy them an ant farm- and a can of Raid. I, however, obviously did not inherit his bug killing genes. Bug killing is not a genetic trait you're no doubt thinking. I would understand your suspicion if I hadn't met Eddie, a third generation bug man.

He showed up at my house with an eerie glee in his eyes. He stood on my porch and explained what he would be doing and he did it with the kind of excitement I've only seen at an amusement park when a child sees a roller coaster. Then he got serious; "I want to see the bugs." With flashlight in hand, he began in the basement, talking, I thought to me. Not so. He was almost in a trance as I explained that we didn't have ants in the basement. They were out on the back deck and the kitchen I tried to tell him. Tried was the operative word because he wasn't listening to me, he was trying to coax the ants out of the insulation.

"Yeah, that there's where you like it don't you? All that nice pink insulation. Hahaha! Well, enjoy your last few minutes fellas! HAHAHA-HAHA!"

Only then did he remember that I was standing there as he spied a "juicy" spider that he made me watch as he pinched it out ... literally pinched it between his thumb and index finger. He gave me the creeps. In the kitchen, things got worse when he found a bunch of them under the lazy susan.

"Hello there! Have I got a surprise for you! Ha-ha-ha-ha! I'm going to make you a nice little treat, yup, just come on up and get it!"

He turned to me, his grin almost maniacal.

"You wanna stay and watch Uncle Eddie kill the bad guys?" He asked me. The hair on the back of my neck stood on end. I declined his kind offer, grabbed my beach bag, and ran.

When I returned a few hours later, there was the horrible stench of death, (or was that bug spray?), and a sticky note on the door; 'Bugs will die completely over the next couple of weeks. (Die completely? Do they linger on the brink of death?) Don't worry if you see a few, but call me if my friends aren't dead by then. I'd love to come back and finish'm off." From, Eddie.

I think I'll buy a can of Raid instead. ☺